Dudley
Rediscovered

"Dudley Countess"

Ned Williams

Uralia Press

Ned Williams

Front cover: *You might be surprised to find a Highland band of girl pipers marching down Stone Street - but that is just the point: Dudley is full if surprises! In this case it's all to do with the links forged between Dudley and Fort William by Bert Bissell (1902-1998); Dudley's great peace campaigner and local legend. The picture was taken by Jasbir, a young member of the Vicar Street Young Men's Bible Class, in 1985, when the class was celebrating its 60th Anniversary..*

Frontispiece: *"Dudley Countess" was a trotting pony owned by Messrs. Evans and Maiden, butchers of 171 High Street, Dudley, photographed in 1908 having won four first prizes at a local event. She was a black "Hackney" mare and was auctioned in 1913 when the business was closed.* (Bill Maiden Collection)

The Black Country Society

The Black Country Society was formed in 1967 under the leadership of the late Dr. John Fletcher. It was formed at a time when the identity of many Black Country communities seemed threatened by local government changes and social trends. At the time the use of the term "Black Country" was often used in a negative way. The Society set out to turn this round, to make local people proud of their Black Country heritage and culture and to make sure this was preserved for future generations to enjoy. The general aims of the Society are to stimulate and share interest in the Black Country: its past, present and future.

The Society now has over 2000 members worldwide and organises a variety of activities, such as meetings at several venues, trips, walks, etc. The Society publishes an excellent quarterly magazine distributed by post to all members.

The Society has a long history of producing its own books, and in 1994 began a fruitful association with Sutton Publishing, now known as The History Press, in which nearly 70 books of local photographs have been published. The Society created a photographic archive that has been deposited within the archives of the Black Country Living Museum. The Society is fully supportive of the latter but should not be confused with the museum's own "Friends" who are focussed on the museum's activities.

Details of the Black Country Society are to be found at: www.blackcountrysociety.co.uk or by writing to BCS, P.O.Box 71, Kingswinford, DY6 9YN

This book is dedicated to Kate Williams
(In 1982 "Cinemas of the Black Country" was
dedicated to Kiran Williams and twenty six years have
elapsed before equal treatment has been achieved!)

Dudley Rediscovered
Published by Uralia Press
23 Westland Road, Wolverhampton, WV3 9NZ

First published: 2008
ISBN 1 898 528 08 X
Printed by: Direct Imaging Limited, Kings Norton.
Further information about the author can be found on his
website: www.nedwilliams.co.uk

Contents

Two photographs chosen to represent what you will find in this book. In turning away from the Castle, Zoo and Market Place this book takes you into some of the byways of Dudley - often poorly recorded by photographers! Thie above picture was probably taken in 1941 from the ground in front of the new Vicar Street Chapel, opposite a fish and chip shop and greengrocer at the top of Martin Hill Street. (See page 75) It is just possible to make out the line of Vicar Street with Cash's general store on the corner of Brooke Street. The gable of Ash Leigh House, in Brooke Street, is visible and survives today.

Below: Although this book regrets the loss of many details of the Dudley landscape it's not all bad news! The "Chapel on the Square", Woodside, has enjoyed a new lease of life with the New Testament Church of God. (See page 88) On 30th August 2008 we see the church being re-opened and rededicated after refurbishment. Rev. Johns and Bishop Jackson, and congregation, look on as a ribbon is cut on the new disabled persons' access ramp.

4

Introduction

Welcome to Dudley! Perhaps you have heard that before, after all there are many books about Dudley. What's so special about this one? The answer is that it is my book about Dudley - it's a production has been a personal act of homage to the Black Country town into which I was catapulted in the Autumn of 1962 as an eighteen-year-old Londoner who had never been to Watford, let alone anywhere north of that point!

Many books about Dudley tell you about castles and hill-top zoos and a long-view of a town's development from Saxon times onwards. This book sets out to discover Dudley in the way the town revealed itself to me. In other words we look around Dudley of the early 1960s, section by section, arranged in the order in which I became acquainted with them - with the exception of the town centre which I leave until near the end. The town I saw was born of the industrial revolution and my historical horizons went back little beyond the early nineteenth century. Only much later did I meet people who could take me back much further - like John Hemingway, the Borough Archaeologist, who spent one very wet Wednesday evening taking a few of us along the High Street to the Market Place to contemplate medieval field boundaries. Later Graham Worton, the Borough Geologist, took me back through a historical time-line that I still find mind-boggling.

What I saw in the early 1960s was a busy thriving town - fairly proud of itself and upbeat about how

Below: The centre of Dudley as seen from the Virgin balloon flying from Dudley Zoo car park in 1997. Here is the main street from 'Bottom Church' to 'Top Church' via the Market Place that forms the core axis of the town. However, this book sets out to look at a Dudley that is more than just its 'centre'. (Malcolm Woodall)

the nineteenth century legacy of the industrial revolution had left it in a bit of a mess, but the twentieth century had been spent very productively cleaning things up! Things had been so cleaned up that I thought at first that industry was something that surrounded Dudley rather than formed part of it. In that I was mistaken, and my trip through Netherton on my very first day in the Black Country should have warned me.

Another mistake was to believe that Dudley had then reached some kind of plateau which would be its permanent state as the capital of the Black Country, or the Jewel in the Black Country's crown. I remember going to the opening of an art exhibition in the Art Gallery and the Mayor told us that Dudley would soon become a university town - the cultural, educational and commercial centre of the West Midlands. (He made no mention of places like Birmingham or Wolverhampton - what had they got to do with it?) I was carried away with this confidence, and everything I had learned in the geography section of my training had taught me that Eve Hill was the centre of England - and therefore probably centre of the Universe! A few more slums to clear, a few new estates and schools to build, some car parks to lay out, some shopping facilities to improve and we would ride on the crest of a wave forever.

What went wrong? Some people think that 1066 was the key date - when Normans came and wrecked a Saxon paradise called Mercia, but it could be that 1966 was the real tipping point! In that year Dudley ceased being the County Borough whose boundaries are observed by this book, and began to take in neighbours. Twelve years later this 'trend' was reinforced and Dudley became the huge Black Country Metropolitan Borough that it is today. Why is this so important? I think its importance is reflected in a conversation that I heard the other day in which a Dudley Councillor was telling his listeners that he thought Dudley was a dump. At first I could hardly believe my ears. Surely it was heretical to describe a place as a dump if you yourself were in some way responsible for running the place. Then I began to understand. This councillor represented some outlying ward of the modern Dudley - a place that would once have been surprised to find itself linked to such a distant town! When he used the term "Dudley" he meant the town

this book describes, not the enlarged borough of the twenty-first century. People who represent the "old Dudley" on the present Dudley Council are, of course, a minority. When the creation of modern local government units is placed alongside the fact that central government has virtually neutered local government anyway, there may be no hope for the salvation of "old Dudley".

The other phenomenon of 1966 was the first rise in the level of unemployment since before the Second World War. Perhaps this was the first warning of the possible de-industrialisation of the Black Country. If we thought this didn't matter because the rise of the service sector would compensate for the loss of industrial jobs, we should have looked more carefully at the behaviour of the service sector. Indications of this could be found in Dudley as the town tried to cope with changing patterns of retailing. The opening of the Churchill Precinct and then the Trident Centre seemed good news at the time and showed that Dudley was keeping abreast of the times even if listed buildings had to be destroyed. The truth was that retailing was becoming so swept away by "change" that it would almost sweep itself from Dudley altogether!

So Dudley, with its bustling market place and 'ideal selection' of chain stores, and spacious car parks, would become the victim of trends way beyond its control, and find itself with a council whose main policy has been to "dither" and whose concern has covered an area far wider than that of the "old Dudley." Forty two years on from 1966 the question of finding a future for the "old Dudley" has yet to be solved.

Therefore this book has a fairly twentieth century focus. I have spent the years from 1962 to 2008 discovering Dudley, delving into its recent past to find explanations, sometimes worrying about the present and future, and then finding that producing this book means I have to re-discover Dudley all over again! One of the reasons I have to 're-discover' it is that I took my eye off the ball. In 1968 I joined the newly created Black Country Society and began a long journey of being interested in the region as a whole. That has now led me full circle, because the more one studies the Black Country the more one becomes aware of the "patchwork" and I find myself coming back to look at the individual patches. This process began for me with the study of Quarry Bank and then Netherton. Now when my attention returns to Dudley I find myself obsessed with sub-dividing it. It must be a parallel to that philosophical experience of trying to comprehend the universe while being driven back to the contemplation of a grain of sand!

So welcome to the bits and pieces of Dudley. Come and look at Eve Hill, wander through the Dock, try to find the boundary between Holly Hall and Woodside, come and be lost in the maze that has replaced the streets of Kates Hill. One of the most useful accessories to bring with you on this journey is a map. One good map of Dudley was drawn about 1835 by J. Treasure of Uttoxeter. I will refer to it a

number of times and a copy can be purchased at the archives. Another useful map is the "Union" map of the 1880s - only available for scrutiny in the archives. It shows much of the Dudley that would have to be swept away in the Twentieth Century. And finally, most useful of all, are the Alan Godfrey maps showing us a 1900s Dudley - close enough to be useful, far enough away to be exotic! Because these maps are clever reductions of large-scale maps they are amazingly useful but we may be the last generation that can relate to them!

Another useful tool is "family history". As you will see in this book, I am old-fashioned enough to be geographical in my approach to understanding places - I want to divide a place up into areas and

Below: Building a new Dudley: Castle Gate Island seen from the Virgin balloon in Summer 1997. Note the parapet of Birmingham Road bridge in the bottom right hand corner - at one time crossing the railway line. Note the former Rosland School site in the top right of the picture. Landmarks like the old bus garage and the football pitch

have been swept away to enable traffic to reach the Dudley Southern Bypass, which opened in 2001. The new road has opened up many new ways of appreciating Dudley, and anyone driving along it is given much 'food for thought' about Dudley's future. There can be no doubt that Dudley faces a 'challenge.' (Malcolm Woodall)

see what's going on in each one. Genealogists come along with another perspective altogether. They join up the dots by making connections based on family. While I might be looking at the distribution of fish and chip shops across a given patch, they are busily comprehending it all by seeing who is related to whom. All this became clearer to me when one or two people began talking to me about Dudley in terms of births, deaths and marriages. In fact, at one stage I wondered if I might understand all the industry and commerce of "old Dudley" if I simply studied enough wedding photos. Add that to my natural interest in "incomers" and their contribution to a place and we may have a whole new picture of Dudley.

The most rewarding part of producing a book is meeting all those who turn up to offer their assistance. In the end people have been so willing to share ideas and information about Dudley that this book has had to wrestle with how to cut things out. Firstly this means I offer a big thank you to those listed in the acknowledgements, and secondly it means that this book may be sowing the seeds of a sequel. Long live an interest in Dudley!

Ned Williams   Summer 2008

————

Below: The Council at work in 1955, watched over by Mayor William Wakeman - in the days when Dudley was administered by Dudley folk. (The Wakeman Collection)

Above: Promoting Dudley: Iris Reed and Margaret Barber - the Keepers of the Fountain. This role was created by the then Town Centre Manager, George Whitehouse, about the time of the Millennium. But good ideas don't necessarily flourish in Dudley - the fountain looks neglected and its keepers still promote the towm but with little official support. (NW)

8

Chapter 1
Eve Hill and Salop Street

In the Autumn of 1962 I found myself making a journey to Dudley, Worcestershire, as an ignorant eighteen year old Londoner in search of a future. My destination was the Teachers' Training College, which at that time was hurriedly trying to expand its capacity to deal with two-year courses that had suddenly become three-year courses. The College was opening late and thus I was able to have a last minute interview just before the term started.

My journey to Dudley was eventful and the interview took a slightly bizarre course but the end result was that I was offered a place and I had fallen in love at first sight with this strange place called The Black Country. Such was my ignorance that I had never even heard of that phrase before, and my headmaster in London had assured me that Worcestershire was filled with rolling hills and fruit orchards.

My first task after accepting the offer of a place at Dudley Training College was to help move furniture into the freshly built Halls of Residence in King Edmund Street, and to assemble desks in the new classrooms. A gang of us worked each morning on these jobs and in the afternoon we were treated to introductory tours of the Black Country in a Bedford Dormobile belonging to Jack Aldiss, the Geography Tutor. I could not believe my good fortune - these trips gave me a wonderful introduction to the area that had so excited me on first acquaintance. Jack was an excellent guide and almost immediately took us to the top of Sedgley Beacon and taught us that on a clear day it was possible to see the Urals. The domes of the Kremlin could be glimpsed glistening in the sun as we gazed eastwards looking for the Urals - knowing that someone on the Urals was gazing westwards and thinking to himself that he could just make out the tower on the top of Sedgley Beacon. Jack also told us that Beacon was pronounced "bacon", and that we would all become "taychers".

By the time the college term began and the rest of the students had arrived, I had already learned much about Dudley and the Black Country, but not really grasped the fact that even a lifetime would not be long enough to know everything about the place. The adventure was only just beginning.

I was given a room on the top floor of St. George's Hall - with a view to the east. Every morning I wit-

Wolverhampton trolleybus no. 424 passes St. James' Church, Eve Hill on 18 February 1967 two weeks before their withdrawal.
Eve Hill is already starting to change. The hairdresser's shop on the corner has already been demolished.
(Graham Sidwell)

Above: Looking towards Dudley town centre from the top of the Eve Hill flats in August 1968. In the centre of the picture is the island by St. James' Church at the point where Himley Road reaches Eve Hill. Salop Street chapel's roof can be seen on the left, and to the right of the spire of 'Top Church' it is possible to make out Britannia Terrace and the Old Dock. (Express & Star)

Below: Salop Street used to begin with John Fletcher's hairdressing shop, carrying a poster for the Clifton, Sedgley, and proceeded along an ancient looking terrace. At the extreme right of the picture are hoardings - behind which used to be St. James' School.
(John Fletcher via Harry Shuker, who lived at No.9, by the bus stop.)

nessed two sunrises. Just after the first sunrise the sun seemed to disappear behind a hazy blanket of smog, and then it would rise again and the haziness would dissolve to reveal landmarks like the cooling towers at Ocker Hill, and the distant skyline of Barr Beacon. The one-inch Ordnance Survey map revealed just how much there was to explore in the scene I could see before me. There were places like Swan Village, where I soon discovered there was more to life than feeding the ducks on the village pond.

The area immediately around the college consisted of Eve Hill and Salop Street, stretching to Shavers End. From Eve Hill, a walk along Wolverhampton Street took us straight to the heart of Dudley. This was the area that could be explored on foot. In January 1963 I would bring my motorbike up to Dudley and could explore further afield but the first expeditions, during the Autumn of 1962 were restricted to Dudley.

As a student, one of the first things to embrace was the vast number of pubs in Eve Hill. Symbolically they stretched from the Old Struggling 'Mon' at the top of Wolverhampton Street to the New Struggling 'Mon' at the far end of Salop Street. Students were not necessarily welcome in all of these, but the Royal Oak was the most used by students as the rear entrance was right next door to the Halls of Residence. The others were used by particular cliques or by those in search of a quiet life or even contact with the "locals". I eventually became very fond of The British Oak.

Salop Street was also the place from which to reach the outside world - by catching the 58 trolleybus to Wolverhampton. Birmingham was like another planet but could be reached by using the 125 bus, or by train, or by adventurous alternative routes such as the 74 bus via West Bromwich, the B87 via Oldbury and the 140 via Blackheath. All these were explored without realisation that some of such trips would pass into history, and should have been savoured more fully.

Even in Salop Street and Wolverhampton Street I was unaware of how quickly the townscape would change and, much to my eternal regret, I failed to take the photographs I would now long to have in front of me. Places that I used regularly I hardly observed and thus I now struggle to reconstruct in my memory.

Just round the corner from The Parade, and starting out down Salop Street was Stockton's Garage. Once I had brought my motorbike to Dudley, I found I needed their help frequently to keep me on the road. I often stood on their premises as they performed some act of mercy on my motorbike, but I never photographed the premises and now feel I have no proper picture of it in my head. A little further down Salop Street was the Post Office which I used regularly as my bank and stationery supplier but once again I neither photographed the place nor stored away any visual impressions. As well as The Royal Oak, there were other pubs on this side of the road; The Unicorn, and The Miners Arms. John Stenson has detailed all the shops in Salop Street in his

Looking along Salop Street towards Eve Hill in the 1960s. The Co-op Butchers can be seen on the right, on the corner of West Street, and the Post Office can be seen opposite - the white-fronted building by the phone box. Next door to the Post Office was a fish and chip shop run by the Smith Family.
In the distance it is just possible to see Stockton's garage with its 'BP' sign.
(Lilian Sheldon)

West Street separates the two premises used by Dudley Co-operative Society in Salop Street. On the left is the butchery, with abattoir behind it. On the right is the shop, No. 16a, where the Co-operative society began in 1872. When this picture was taken, in about 1968, the plot on the right was vacant, and was followed by the Salop Street Chapel. In the background the cranes have began work on the Eve Hill flats.
(Roger Crombleholme)

booklet, "Do You Remember?" - his very choice of title making me feel guilty about having to say, "No!" Perhaps our lives in the college were too self-contained to make much use of so many shops - a microcosm of the world of local shops that has now faded away.

Not far from The Miners Arms was a little toy shop run by Emily Parsons, at 120 Salop Street. A few years later I was to meet Emily's son, Harold Parsons, in his role as editor of "The Blackcountryman". Eventually I read his tale of life behind the shop in Salop Street, from 1923 to 1948, in his autobiography: "Substance and Shadow". But of the shop itself, I have no recollection.

My memory of the far side of Salop Street is equally vague. St. James' Infant School, of 1842 vintage, was on this side of the road, not far from the Eve Hill island. This building has now been rebuilt at the Black Country Living Museum - thus compensating me for my poor memory. I wish I had taken more notice of the Co-op butchers next door to the school, and on the corner of West Street, and further on was the Co-op Grocery. The butchers shop, and the abattoir behind it are the focus of several Eve Hill folk tales, and the Co-op Grocery was of more historical importance than I could have imagined.

In the early 1990s I became very interested in the history of the Co-op Movement and began work on a book about local Co-operative Societies that would mark the 150th anniversary of the Movement in 1994. The history of the Dudley Society was particularly difficult to research as so many records had been lost when the Society was absorbed by the Birmingham Society in 1982. As it turns out, the Dudley Co-operative Society began life in Salop Street. It was founded in 1872 by illiterate nail-makers desperate to alleviate their poverty. They opened their first shop at 16a Salop Street in the October of that year, and took £27 during the first week of trading. Later the Society moved its headquarters to New Street and then to Waddhams Pool. Expansion and financial problems followed in the 1890s, but the little shop in Salop Street survived to be around at the time of the Society's centenary in 1972 but closed soon afterwards. Needless to say, I neglected to photograph it.

Between the two Co-op premises was the Salop Street Methodist Chapel. How I could miss a chapel, I don't know - but somehow I did! I have no recollection of the building at all. In the early years of the 21st Century I have become involved in a major study of local chapels but in the 1960s they must have been invisible to me. Perhaps my excuse could be that Salop Street Chapel was in the process of closing and merging with "Central" just at the time I was first exploring my new home in Eve Hill.

On the stretch of Salop Street between Dudley Street and Peel Street was another pub, this one rejoiced in the name, "The Welsh Go By". The name

Right: Salop Street Wesleyan Methodist Chapel was opened in 1849 and survived until 1965, when its congregation merged with Wesley, King Street, and Wellington Road, to form "Central" in Wolverhampton Street. This picture was printed on the front page of the last order of service.
The building was demolished in 1968.

Below: We see the interior of this chapel, photographed during the Sunday School Anniversary of June 1949. Rev. Frank Bowyer is in the pulpit and the organist, in open-necked shirt, just to the right of the console, is Harry Shaw.

(Both photographs supplied by F.B.Shaw)

was thought to be connected to the ancient existence of "drovers' trails" from Wales to the West Midlands. A few yards away, on the corner of Peel Street was the "Sir Robert Peel", and across the road was "The British Oak". On Sunday evenings the British Oak was crowded and singing replaced the usual ritualistic playing of dominoes. A comedy turn was provided by Bill Cotton who raised a laugh by imitating the accents of the regulars of the surrounding pubs. It was a lesson in the subtleties of the Black Country accent and dialect - a language that changed every hundred yards!

Beyond the British Oak, on the site of the present Christian Fellowship buildings and its car park were some houses and an entry that at one time provided access to a yard and the Bethel Temple. This "temple" was another product of the Jeffreys' Crusade that came to Dudley in 1930. It was led by a Mr. Hall and pastored by Rev.Thrush. Ironically another Pentecostal assembly became established on the opposite side of Salop Street, led by Pastor Joseph Giles. It was that congregation that crossed the road in the 1970s and opened the present Christian Fellowship - absorbing the last few survivors of the Bethel as it did so.

Beyond the Fellowship, and Windmill Street, a few houses of "old Salop Street" still stand - set back from Salop Street and built on higher ground.

Windmill Street itself climbs very steeply onto this high ground - once known as the Mill Bank - home to allotments and a late nineteenth century football pitch carved out of the pit-banks. The windmill is shown on the 1865 maps of Dudley, but had gone by the end of the century. The football pitch was the home of Dudley Football Club until the club moved to the Birmingham Road cricket ground in 1911. After that date the Shavers End pitch was used by the Dudley Phoenix Football Club!

The banks sloped down to Dibdale Road, once known as Bagley's Lane, and at this point "The New Struggling Man" marks the end of Salop Street and the beginning of Dudley's frontier settlement of Shaver's End. This little settlement that sprang up in the 1860s and 1870s, stretched from Nith Place to the Reservoir, along Highland Road - beyond which the road entered the Urban District of Sedgley.

In the late 1960s, and into the 1970s, the Salop Street described here plus West Street, Dudley Street, Peel Street and St. James's Terrace, were all demolished and a vast area was cleared to make way for the construction of the Eve Hill tower-blocks. The trolleybuses had ceased running along Salop Street in March 1967, and even the other side of Salop Street began to disappear to prepare for the expansion of the College, or was it the much rumoured widening of Salop Street itself? Two out of the three tower-blocks were demolished in 1999 and a new "Salop Street community" of modern houses has been built on the site of the "village" destroyed thirty years earlier.

Above left: The Brtish Oak on the out-of-town corner of Peel Street, in October 1970. It appears to have a history stretching back to the 1850s, once again testifying to the early development of this stretch of road. Eventually it became the only building on the western side of Salop Street to remain standing even although it finally closed as a pub after a short independent career of about ten years.(It had ceased to be an Ansells pub in 1984.) Today the building has become an annexe of the new Christian Fellowship built next door. "Under New Management" - as their sign used to say. (NW)

Above right: The Robert Peel, also photographed in October 1970 when in an advance stage of demolition. Behind the pub stands one of the three Eve Hill tower-blocks: Butterfield Court - the only surviving one. (NW)

Right: Looking across Salop Street past the corner of the British Oak in October 1970 showing the run-down state of the eastern side of the road by that time. (NW)

Looking back down Salop Street towards Eve Hill in the 1960s. (Lilian Sheldon)

Looking along the eastern side of Salop Street, looking towards Eve Hill, in October 1970 while the buildings on this side of the road were being demolished by H.J.Cooper of Dudley. On the extreme right is the remains of The Unicorn public house. Note the top of the college Halls of Residence behind the buildings in Salop Street. (NW)

Looking down the western side of an empty Salop Street in 1962.
Note the entry slightly right of centre: this provided access to the small Bethel Mission established after Edward Jeffreys' crusade of 1930. The British Oak and Robert Peel are just left of centre.
(A. Simcox via Lilian Sheldon)

The Miners Arms, on the east side of Salop Street in the 1960s. To the right of this picture there had been open ground which was used by the Dudley Pentacostal Church to build their hall in 1949, having used an upper room in Cross Street since about 1934 when they first formed.
(Dudley Archives via Lilian Sheldon)

The Dudley Pentacostal Church of 1949 vintage, led by Pastor Giles - seen on the extreme right. The congregation crossed Salop Street in the mid 1970s to their present hall.
(Mavis Ainsbury)

The British Oak has now become an annexe of the new Dudley Christian, which can be seen on the right hand side of the picture. The new centre was opened on 3rd April 1976 - by Kath Giles - the widow of Pastor Joseph Giles who had led the fellowship in 1949. Windmill Street joins Salop Street just beyond the centre.
(NW)

The "fruit and veg" shop belonging to John and Clara Jewkes of 123 Salop Street as it was in about 1910. The family appear to have been joined by a pet sheep in this picture!

John and Clara's daughter Anne, who may be on the left of this picture, married Tom Maiden on 29th October 1917 thus bringing together a dynasty of greengrocers with a dynasty of butchers.

In later years 123 Salop Street became the property of Absolom Bunn, known locally as "Happy Bunn" - fruiterer and poulterer.

(From the Collection of Bill Maiden)

Left: 120 Salop Street forms the centrepiece of this photo and was the toy/hardware shop run by Emily Parsons - the mother of Harold Parsons, gag writer, professional journalist and first editor of The Blackcountryman. Harold took the picture just after his mother retired in 1951.

To the left is Harold Edward's newsagency. To the right of the entry are Raybould's drapery and Roland Armishaw's bakery.

(Harold Parsons, BCS Collection)

An interior view at the bar of The British Oak, taken in 1969. On the right is Bill Cotton, a local resident who could mimic the slight variations to Black Country speech to be found in each of Salop Street's pubs. (NW)

Wolverhampton Corporation Transport no.73 (7073 UK) a Guy Arab V of 1962 vintage passes the "High Side" houses in Salop Street in the late 1960s. The houses on the right still survive and the little shop has been refurbished although not currently used for retailing.
The buildings on the left were finally swept away when Wolverhampton University wanted to provide a large car park for its Dudley Campus. (Paul Roberts)

The "High Side" houses can be seen once again in this photograph taken on Sunday 18th July 1999 to record the demolition by controlled explosion of two of the Eve Hill tower blocks. The picture was taken from an extension roof of the Salamander pub - now a Chinese restaurant! Butterfield Court, on the right is the only remaining tower. (NW)

The Struggling Man pub at the end of Salop Street. The main road then becomes Highland Road for a short stretch as it passes through the border village of Shaver's End. Once across the boundary and into Sedgley UDC the road becomes Burton Road. To the right Dibdale Road heads for the Gornals. (NW)

Shaver's End about 1910 as seen from The Struggling Man, with Dibdale Road in the fore-ground. In recent years the 'V' of the junction was occupied by the Highland Garage selling Esso petrol. This has now been replaced with a filling station and Tesco supermarket. Modern flats occupy the far side of the road next door to The Salamander, but many of the houses in the distance still stand. The slightly higher one in the far distance, right on the Sedgley boundary, dates from 1865 - the year Dudley became a modern borough.
(Ken Rock Collection)

As one leaves Tesco Express, seen here on 8th. February 2008, one steps back into nineteenth century Dudley for the last few yards to the border with Sedgley. "Ogley Hay Cottage" in the background carries an 1878 building date. We return to Shaver's End in a later chapter to take account of a few Dudley landmarks right on this border - eg. the reservoirs, and the workhouse come hospital at Burton Road. (NW)

Chapter 2
Wolverhampton Street

During my first year in Dudley (1962/63) Eve Hill was on my doorstep, but Wolverhampton Street was close to hand. From our base in King Edmund Street, we could make for the centre of Dudley via St. James's Road or via Wolverhampton Street - two very contrasting thoroughfares. Wolverhampton Street was reached via Eve Hill itself - that crest of the ridge where St. James' Church had been built in 1840. We enjoyed the legend that children reciting the Lords Prayer in this building would say, "Deliver us from Eve Hill", and we had no reason to doubt it. We were also told that Salop Street was the principal water-shed of England and that water entering the drains on the eastern side of the road descended to the Tame and then to the Trent and the Humber and out into the North Sea, whereas water entering drains on the other side of the road formed streams that eventually joined the Stour and thence to the Severn and via the Bristol Channel to the Atlantic.

Wolverhampton Street was numbered from its junction with the Market Place and High Street - with numbers coming up the road to Eve Hill on the left hand side, starting with Hollins' shop at no.1 and returning on the opposite side. Following the logic of this numbering scheme Wolverhampton Street ended where it began, but to me Wolverhampton Street began at the point where I passed St. James' Church. Almost immediately one encountered a drive that led to Gorton's Rope Works - how I wish I had explored it or at least had stopped to find out if it was still in business. On the other side of the drive was The Star Inn which had probably ceased to be an inn way back in 1934. The front of the rope-works separated The Star from The Old Struggling Man.

The next drive was known as Noisy Row and a fish and chip shop stood on the corner, and from then on little shops came thick and fast - now replaced with more modern shops set back from the street. These modern shops contain businesses that maintain a connection to the past - both the hairdresser, and the flower shop, of 2008 are "descended" from businesses in the old Wolverhampton Street.

From 102 Wolverhampton Street onwards was a "parade" style building which began with a pharmacy (once "Walker's"), a small shop that had once sold carpets, and a butcher's (Richard Miles), and continued to include the Davenports "Beer at Home" premises. The building, centred on 118 Wolverhampton Street, has an impressive frontage. The Davenports section has become home to a new Apostolic church.

St. James' Church, Eve Hill, photographed in 2007. It was built in 1840 and became centre of its own parish on 15th October 1844. It has been described as being built in the "Early English" style. Most noticeably it is a "twin" to St. John's Church built at the same time in Kates Hill. A chancel, organ and vestry were added in 1869.

The church was substantially refurbished in 1906 when the surrounding wall of Gornal stone was added. Work was so substantial that the church closed briefly only to be re-opend on 25th July 1906. (NW)

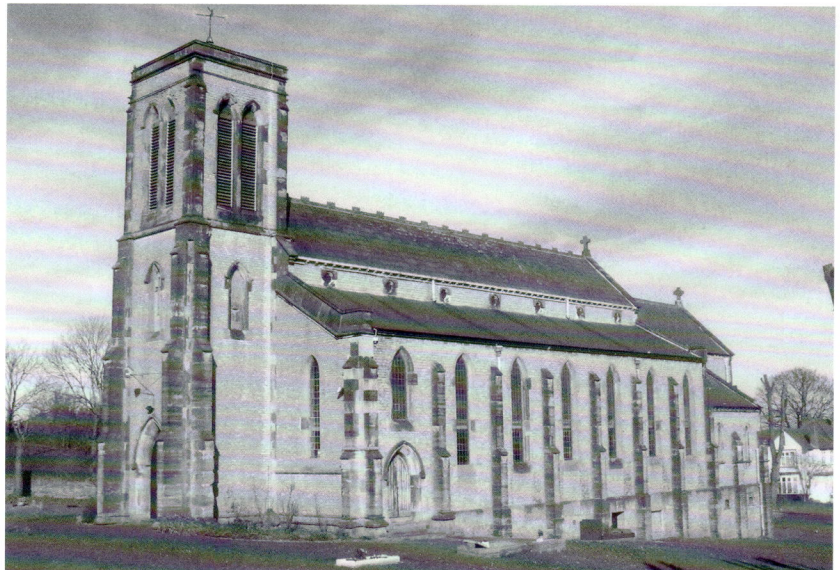

Left: The interior of St. James' Church, Eve Hill, photographed on Mothering Sunday 2008. The light airy interior is finished in white and blue and succesfully combines size with intimacy even when viewed from the back of the balcony. (NW)

The Star Inn, Wolverhampton Street, photographed in the 1930s. The church wall is seen on the left, separated from the pub by an entry which provided access to Gorton's Rope Works. Note the electric traction pole with its heavy cast iron base. At the time this photograph was taken the electric trams on the Wolverhampton - Dudley route had been replaced with trolley buses. (NW)

The Davenports Building in Wolverhampton Street, in its contemporary guise as head quarters of the Revival Fires Apostolic Resource Centre, opened in 2005.

Davenport's brewery was in Bath Row, Birmingham and they had been brewing beer there since 1885. They developed a special trade in doorstep deliveries of bottled beer for home consumption - built up by Baron John Davenport, son of the original brewer. Depots like these were established to make such deliveries possible.

(NW)

Beyond Davenports were more small shops and houses - Sam Foleys' Fruit and Veg, Piggott's Sweets and Tobacco (122), Harold Dews, the Butchers (123/124) and Alice Morgan's general store. There were several little shops in this stretch that had been converted from the front rooms of houses. Another pub was to be found at "The Duke of York", also known as "The Duck Pen". In my time the next shop was Midland Wallpapers (see the 1968 photograph below) but this had once been Walter Fisher's fried fish shop. Next door at 131 had been Timmins' boot and shoe shop, where they also sold toys, but by the 1960s this had become Marsh's hardware store. This whole stretch has disappeared and been replaced with Chaddesley Court old peoples' flats giving this part of Wolverhampton Street a quiet residential aspect.

140 Wolverhampton Street stood on the corner of The Belper and had once been Broome's, formerly Jackson's, drapery and babywear shop. The Belper always seemed an interesting side-street - its unusual name suggesting a connection with Derbyshire nailers who may have come to Dudley in the early nineteenth century. A pleasant Victorian terrace still occupies one side of The Belper today, but at one time it seemed to provide access to a track that went through to St. James's Road and also provided access to Reynolds & Hughes bakery and Guest's coal yard.

On the town centre side of The Belper Wolverhampton Street resumed its steady succession of shops. In the 1960s a fishmonger was followed by a butcher, and it was here that I was sold my first encounter with faggots. Both shops were associated with the Westwood family. At 143 Wolverhampton Street was Gordon Smith's greengrocery. I became better acquainted with this shop during the 1980s and Gordon Smith explained that it had been passed on to him from his mother and father, Nellie and George Smith. The latter had turned the premises into a greengrocery after the First World War, and his son felt that it had altered very little during the past sixty years up until the 1980s. Since then it has closed and the handsome building has returned to domestic use.

W. Davies & Son had a grocery next to Smith's shop, and on the far side of an entry one came to Sherratt's Radio Shop at 145. It had been a radio shop since the earliest days of crystal sets, and before the coming of domestic electricity the family had sold lamp oil. The tall building that today hosts a Chinese "take-away" ("China Express") was once the shop attached to Reynolds & Hughes' Bakery, and was later used by Robinson's, the West Bromwich-based bakers.

Below: Wolverhampton Street below Davenports premises in April 1968. The Duke of York can be seen behind the two-tone Wolsley (NW)

Above: A Victorian terrace in The Belper in 2007: a quiet tributory off Wolverhampton Street. Note the new houses in the background where Reynolds & Hughes' Bakery once stood. Nailors from Derbyshire may have brought the "Belper" name with them. (NW)

Below: George Smith's greengrocery shop is in the centre of this view along Wolverhampton Street taken in 1968. The Belper is on the left. Note the trolleybus traction pole and the Odeon and Gaumont advertising boards - the latter completely blank by 1968. (NW)

Right: George Smith's fruit and veg shop at 143 Wolverhampton Street photographed on a Sunday in about 1985. On a weekday the blinds would be down and some stock would be displayed outside the front of the shop. By this time the shop was being run by George's son: Gordon Smith. George was of the opinion that his father acquired the premises just after the First World War, and before that time it may have been a butcher's shop belonging to Charles Readdy. (NW)

Below: This 2007 view illustrates the fact that Gordon Smith has now retired and the premises have returned to exclusively domestic use. Sherratt's radio and electrical shop (at 145) has become Countrywide doors and conservatories and the lofty building at 146 has become China Express while the shop next door has disappeared altogether. (NW)

Behind these buildings had been the bakery usually associated with Mssrs. Reynolds and Hughes. However, in the early years of the 20th century, nos. 144 and 145 Wolverhampton Street were occupied by Mr. Solomon Rhodes, a grocer who appears to have started a rival bakery in Stafford Street. The latter was sold in the 1920s to W. Price & Sons - producers of "Daily Bread"! What with Mr. Davies' bakery in Wellington Road - there was no shortage of bakeries. (NW)

Above: A horse-drawn tank of lamp oil pauses outside James Anyon's shop at 158 Wolverhampton Street about 1910. Note the range of lamp fittings on show in Anyon's window. There is a family connection here between James Anyon and H. A. Sherratt who later traded at 145 Wolverhampton Street. (His initials stood for Hugh Anyon) (Bytheway Collection)

Right: H.A. Sherratt shares advertising space with Reynolds & Hughes' Bakery in a 1935 directory.

John Gray's horse-drawn delivery van of about 1910 carries the address as 178 Wolverhampton Street, a shop opposite the entry to Tinchbourne Street usually associated with Williams' Grocery store at that time and later with George Marsh. John Gray, as a wholesaler, collected sweets from the "cottage-based" suppliers, and built the business which became Teddy Gray's. (Gray Colln.)

T. A. CLARKE.

NOTED FOR SOUND RELIABLE

~ FURNITURE

At Astonishingly Low Prices.

Cabinet Makers, Upholsterers, and French Polishers sent any distance for

— RENOVATIONS —
on receipt of Post Card.

Furniture Removals a Speciality.

146, Wolverhampton Street,
Factory: WELLINGTON ROAD, DUDLEY.

A Wolverhampton Street Miscellany: Above: Mr. Clarke's 1905 advertisement reminds us of the full range of goods and services available along this street. Below: The Davenport's Buildings - flanking the entry to their yard seen in 1968 when Grange Crafts were at 116. (NW)

Above: The pharmacy at 113 Wolverhampton Street in 1968. This 1930s 'parade' consisted of four shops then the entry created by the demolition of 117, followed by 118 seen below. (NW)

148 Wolverhampton Street about 1910 with Isaac Whitehouse, shoemaker and repairer, standing in the doorway. The shop later sold sweets and then became a cobblers once again. (Bytheway Collection)

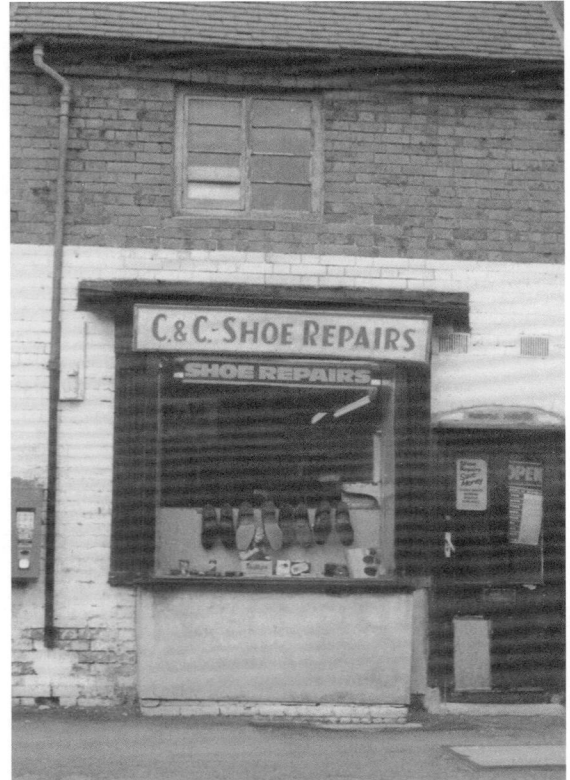

C&C Shoe Repairs at 148 Wolverhampton Street in April 1988. In the 1930s it had been occupied by Charles Abraham, but by the sixties it belonged to Dennis Clark. (NW)

At 148 was one of Wolverhampton Street's cobblers; Charles Abraham, followed by premises eventually used by Arthur Parkes, a radio engineer who had earlier worked for Sherratt's of Wolverhampton Street. Another entry and a few yards on and we came to George Bytheway's newsagency at 150. I got to know George's son Donald Bytheway as we had a common interest in trains and Donald had an interesting collection of shop photographs as well as a knowledge of the history of the family business. One such picture was taken outside the pub next door: "The Fox" where Joe Wade had once produced his own beer.

More small premises followed: George Lacy at 154, who sold sweets and tobacco, and Joseph Kendall using 155 as a private residence. 156 was another little cobbler's shop, this one had been run by Sam Smart. Mitchell's Fruit and Veg was at 157 and Elizabeth Blissett at 159 selling wallpaper. Around this point was Blewitt's book shop at 157 - to which

we were sent by the Teacher Training College to purchase books from our reading list.

Opposite Chapel Street, later known as Charlton Street was Round's Corn shop which sold pet food and goldfish as well as "corn". By the time I knew these premises they were owned by Dudley Factors. This business had been started by Oliver Bevan and his wife Ruby, who was connected to the Dancer family of Halesowen. Later their son David came into the business and it gradually expanded into surrounding premises - all packed with "parts". The business was taken over by Quentin Hazell, later becoming Partco. A move followed to the other side of Wolverhampton Street to the original premises of North Worcester Garages. It eventually closed when Partco became Unipart.

George Westwood was once at 160 with a sweets and picture-framing, next door to the Case Sisters' drapery shop (161). 162 was George Wainwright's cycle shop, but to complicate matters Wainwrights later occupied 164. Number 164 was at the end of a Victorian terrace and was immediately followed by a small block of older buildings probably dating back to the eighteenth century. (165, 166 and 167) John Burgin dates them to 1795 and thinks they became shops in the 1850s. Before Wainwrights took over 164 it had been Edith Whiston's Music Shop. Madam Whiston taught the piano and ran an accordion band. At some stage she sold the business to William Hand, best known as the Musical Director at Dudley Hippodrome.

165-167 form an interesting threesome. Up until the First World War the block had belonged to Hayden's, who were fish sellers. Then the buildings were bought by Alfred Burgin whose father John Burgin Senior had started the business at 167 in 1868. In 1881 he added a printing press to a building at the rear of the shop and they became pioneer booksellers, stationers, newsagents and printers. However, we haven't reached 167 yet! For many years 165 was a gents' hairdresser, first run by Edgar Burton and then Jack Tombs. Today it is a record shop. No.166 for the last twenty years has been occupied by a catering business but at one time

it had been Benjamin Westwood's top quality fish shop. He had taken the business over from Mr. Hayden who had owned the block of three shops.

At last we come to Burgin's News Agency - celebrating 140 years in the business during 2008! This shop has been one of the great survivors of Wolverhampton Street as such a record suggests. John Burgin who is running the shop during its 140th year is the grandson of his namesake who founded it in 1868. (See page 43) At this point we can pause for breath in this relentless procession of small shops as their flow is interrupted by the one-time presence of the Wolverhampton Street schools, standing opposite the commencement of Southall's Lane. We will explore the latter when we make our way back along the other side of Wolverhampton Street.

Below: George Bytheway's shop at 150 Wolverhampton Street in November 1937. This picture makes an interesting comparsion with a slightly later photograph I reproduced in the 1989 publication: "Black Country Folk at Werk" which included the transcript of an interview with Donald Bytheway. (Bytheway Collection)

Shops resumed as soon as we passed Wolverhampton Street School, with no.172, once occupied by Walker's chemist shop. Next door, at 173, was Ernest Jewke's tiny cobblers shop. Ernest Jewkes described himself as a clogger but demand for clogs had declined by the time I came to explore Wolverhampton Street and only a shoe-repairing business remained. More significant to Dudley folk was the poultry and flower shop at 174. This was run by the Hooper Family, involved in the local swimming scene, but best known by their association with Billy Dainty. Billy was actually born on the opposite side of Wolverhampton Street, but spent much of his youth at Hooper's, and at some stage he had played the ukulele with Whiston's Accordian Band.

The musical connections extended to Mrs. Streele's drapery, next door to Hooper's, because her husband played the banjo. No. 176 had once been premises used by George Harvey, a furniture maker and violinist, and before that it had been Arthur Williams' grocery store. At this point there was a small entry, beyond which was a two-part building once owned by George Marsh. He operated a tobacconists in 177 and a bakery selling home-baked bread in 178. More little shops followed including premises (at 180) which became Gill & Jones, the printers.

Somewhere at this point one came to the imposing premises of the Royal Liver Insurance Company, managed in pre-war days by Samuel Littler. (The Royal Liver was established in Liverpool in 1850 as

Left: Hooper's Flower Shop at 174 Wolverhampton Street decorated for the Coronation in 1953. Mr. & Mrs. Hooper had two daughters: Florence and Ada, who were expert florists. Ada was the mother of Billy Dainty, the famous dancer and comedian, born just across the road on the corner of Southall's Lane in 1927. Like many other local people, Billy began his musical education in Mrs. Whiston's music classes and accordian band. He and John Burgin, born within a fortnight of each other, were both taught by Mrs. Whiston - John on mandolin and Billy on ukulele. (Bill Boyd)

a Friendly Society which would provide decent burial for its members - and is still a 'mutual' organisation today.) Some more little shops followed until reaching the premises of Dicken's the heating engineers, who occupied the site on the corner of Trinity Road. From the top of Trinity Road one looked across Wolverhampton Street to the Wesley Methodist Chapel which we will consider on our return. To the left once stood the Presbyterian Church which had been destroyed by fire in June 1944. When the church had been built almost a century earlier, in 1847, it was on the outskirts of Dudley. The congregation retreated after the fire to their church hall until a new church could be built in Trinity Road in 1949. Both the hall and the replacement church, now "United Reform" still stand today.

From Trinity Road to Parson's Street, Wolverhampton Street took on a different character. Having once been the outer suburbs of Dudley it was graced with large houses which eventually became the offices of solicitors and accountants, and other 'professionals'. The first, at 188, was the surgery of Dr. Vivian Gray Maitland, and later Dr. John MacDonald. Two doors away at 190 was Frank Morris, the dentist.

191 was set back from the road but at some stage had joined with 192, which conformed to the general building line at this point. The premises belonged to Benjamin Whittaker, an electrical engineer. 193 was an equally large house used by Alfred Wright Dando - estate agent and solicitor. 195 formed the corner building on reaching Parson's Street and in pre-war days was the office of another solicitor: Jabez Round.

Parson's Street later developed great personal significance for me because it housed the Dudley Employment Exchange where I worked from October 1966 until the following summer. On the corner of Parson's Street and Wolverhampton Street closest to the town centre was Chaddesley House used by the solicitors Wall and Tanfield, followed by further impressive Georgian buildings now inhabited by solicitors and accountants until reaching the General Post Office building on the corner of Priory Street. This was a late Edwardian building that once always seemed so busy that nobody could ever imagine it might one day close.

From the corner of Priory Street to the centre of Dudley, Wolverhampton Street changed character once again and became part of the town-centre. This was heralded by the Crown public house at 201. The loftiness of this building was reminiscent of London Edwardian pubs and therefore we should not be surprised to find that the building replaced an older building which had previously occupied the site.

Left: Trinity Presbyterian Church which at once stood on the corner of Wolverhampton Street and Trinity Road.
Below: Georgian twon houses that have become offices on the stretch of Wolverhampton Street between Parson's Street and Priory Street. (NW)

Dudley Central Methodist Church, once known as "The Wesley", awaiting demolition, in the mid 1970s, and replacement - separated from Wolverhampton Street by this rising burial ground. It started life in 1829 as a Wesleyan chapel but defected to the New Connexion. Such 'differences' lost their meaning in the 1930s but it took until the 1960s for real mergers to take place.
From this vantage point one now looks through trees to the new building which, from this elevation, looks like a grey slate-covered pyramid!
(Joyce Round)

Shops follow in such profusion it is impossible to name them all although one or two can be singled out for special mention. For example Lillian Stainton's ladies' wear shop at 203 was distinctly up-market. Famous visiting female artistes from Dudley Hippodrome were known to visit this shop. The huge glass-fronted furniture store belonging to the Worcestershire Furnishing Company was a fine example of Edwardian iron-framed construction exploiting huge areas of plate glass to admit light to its showrooms. It filled plots no.s 211, 212 and 213 of Wolverhampton Street, and was later known as Goodly's.

The Wolverhampton Street numbering system actually ended at 224, adjacent to the corner building once another elaborate Edwardian building, but now replaced with something more modern and occupied by W.H.Smith. Having reached this point we can turn round and explore Wolverhampton Street's left hand side making our way back to Eve Hill. The journey begins with John Hollin's jewellery shop at no.1. This magnificent Edwardian shop front has survived to the present day and is well worth an inspection. However, progress along Wolverhampton street reveals that very little else has been preserved and an entrance to the car parks

Dudley Head Post Office built on the corner of Wolverhampton Stret and Priory Street, 27th September 1984.

This building was opened in 1909 replacing an earlier one on the same site.
(Keith Hodgkins)

Above: The Crown Inn on the corner of Wolverhampton Street and Priory Street, October 1985. (NW)
Below: Wolverhampton Street looking towards High Street in the 1940s. Mrs. Stainton's dresswear shop on the left at 203. (Ken Rock Collection)

Above: A 1903 picture of the Worcestershire Furnishing Company's glass-fronted store at 211 - 213 Wolverhampton Street, next door to the office of the Dudley Herald. Nothing of this survives. (Dudley Archives)

Left: The view of Wolverhampton Street from its junction with High Street, as portrayed by a "Lilywhite" post card of the early 1920s. The shoe shop of Messrs Freeman, Hardy & Willis stood on the left hand corner until the 1970s. The building on the right is illustrated on the opposite page, and has now been replaced with a branch of W.H. Smith. Beyond the shoe shop on the left you can see Hollin's jewelery shop and the Hanson's pub: The Talbot Inn.
(Ken Rock Collection)

Left: Hollins' jewelery shop at 1 Wolverhampton Street. The business traced its history back to 1804 and probably began in King Street. By the 1900s the shop in Wolverhampton Street looked like this but was then given a dramatic Edwardian "makeover" - seen on the next page. The nameboard was subsequently raised - as can be seen in the above picture.
(John Hollins' Collection)

Left: Alex Young & Son, tailors, at 22 Wolverhampton Street. Their advert claimed, "Splendid value in blue serge suits, uniforms, clerical garments and liveries a speciality.". They were on this site until the Second World War, but then moved to Stone Street. A Kentucky Fried Chicken fast-food outlet now uses this 'end-site' of the town-centre section of Wolverhampton Street.
(Bill Boyd)

Above: The shop on the corner of Wolverhampton Street and High Street is actually 209/210 High Street, and in its modern form is occupied by W.H.Smith. Looking at the lofty Edwardian building once on the site we can see it complemented the architecture of The Crown Inn. When "new" this was occupied by Thomas Williams, glover, clothier and gents' outfitter. When photographed in October 1978 it had been occupied by Burton's. (Keith Hodgkins)

Top right: John Hollins' shop at 1 Wolverhampton Street as rebuilt about 1910, with magnificent carved and gilded nameboard, and a host of shop-front details which were fashionbale at the time.

Thankfully this frontage, minus the gilding and the wrought iron work, has been preserved. (John Hollins' Collection)

Far Right: An advert of 1905 vintage.

Right: The shop today. (NW)

WATCHES .

CLOCKS . .

BRONZES . . .

. Silver and
Silver-plated Goods
SUITABLE FOR . .

Presentations.

JOHN HOLLINS
JEWELLER,
1, Wolverhampton Street, Dudley.

The Cheapest House in the District for

Diamond Engagement Rings

22-carat Guinea Gold Wedding Rings,
Birthday Presents and Useful Wedding Presents.

Largest Stock in the Midlands.   Everything marked
. in plain figures.

1, WOLVERHAMPTON STREET,
Also 27, 28 & 29, KING STREET, DUDLEY.

Left: Finch's House - the home of Joseph and Mary Finch, at 30 Wolverhampton Street, bears the date 1707. The Finch family in Dudley can be traced back at least until Elizabethan times, and when they built this elegant house in 1707 it was on the outskirts of town. Joseph's grandson, John Finch, is credited with opening the first bank in Dudley. (NW)

beneath the Trident Centre reminds us of 'modernisation' that has generally erased 'character' from the town centre.

Life becomes more interesting as we approach the junction with Priory Street. Tucked away behind nos. 20 - 22 are the buildings that make up the complex belonging to the old Unitarian Meeting House and its Sunday School. The chapel, representing very early non-conformity in Dudley, with a history going back to the early eighteenth century, was a victim of the Sacheverall riots of 1715 and was subsequently rebuilt. Although it enjoyed various restorations and refurbishments, it does not look healthy today.

Opposite Priory Street was Horsley House, once the home of Alderman Herbert William Hughes, a mining engineer who had been Mayor of Dudley in 1920/21. Next door, at nos. 25/26 was Lloyd's Bank,

The Mechanics Institute was founded in 1848 and was greatly extended to look like this in 1863. The hall was built with funds collected from the organisation of the Castle fetes. It provided adult education, a geological museum and a large public hall. The latter was later used as a cinema and later still as a ballroom. This picture was used in Blocksidge's Guide of 1905 which contained a history of the Institute. (Mr. Blocksidge had just become the librarian of the Institute.)

followed by Finch House, once again reminding us of the Georgian expansion of Dudley and the creation of a "suburb" along Wolverhampton Street. Crossing Inhedge one passed another dentist's practice and came to the Mechanics Institute. When I became acquainted with Wolverhampton Street in the 1960s, this was mysteriously boarded up giving no clues to its interesting history. The story included its part in the provision of adult education in Dudley, its "public hall" was Dudley's first 'proper' cinema thanks to the efforts of one Irving Bosco, and in later years it had housed a ballroom developed by the Kennedy Family of Hippodrome fame. A few doors away was the wonderfully named "British Working Men's Café", which in the 1960s I knew as "Robo's" - home of the tasty bacon or sausage sandwich.

What went on behind the buildings that faced this part of Wolverhampton Street is obscure. There had been some old Victorian "courts" that seem to have survived at least until the 1950s. Hartland's the decorators occupied no.35 Wolverhampton Street - often illustrated in the Blocksidge's Almanacs of the first part of the twentieth century. At 37, on the corner of Gads Lane, was Joseph Badley's hardware shop. In the Wolverhampton Street tradition, Mr. Badley was also a musician and could teach both piano and violin.

Gads Lane had once been known as Dog Lane according to Treasure's map of Dudley, and had at one time been the location of a Council Depot which had been home to Dudley Council's first steam roller. On the out-of-town side of Gads Lane were the grounds of the Wolverhampton Street Methodist Church - standing well back from the street on rising ground. During the 1960s I used to feel that it looked rather forlorn and bedraggled - even rather lonely in the way it was set back so far from the street. It was difficult to believe that this ground had once been packed with people on 2nd September 1937 when Dorothy Round, Dudley's tennis heroine married Dr. Little at the chapel. The building had an interesting history going back to an opening in 1829 when it had been built by Wesleyan Methodists expanding from their base in King Street. There was a "falling out" in 1835 and the congregation decided to merge with the New Connexion. It became an important representative of the New Connexion and on at least three occasions hosted the denomination's annual conference. It was also Dudley's first chapel to be lit by electricity - as early as 1889.

The New Connexion Methodists built a large Sunday School building in 1859 almost next door to their chapel, but its frontage faced Tinchbourne Street. To add to the confusion it was often called the Rose Hill Sunday School. When the local Methodist chapels had to "rationalise" in the 1960s, congregations regrouped in Wolverhampton Street using the name "Central". The last service was held at "Central" in 1973 but demolition was delayed. Its modern replacement opened on 16th September 1978.

Rather curiously the area next door to the chapel, occupying the corner of Tinchbourne Street, became a Regent petrol station, perhaps obscuring what had been there earlier. The Vine - a typical Black Country pub, occupied the other corner of Tinchbourne Street with a central entrance between two shallow bays. For many years the landlord was Tom Butcher, another well-known Wolverhampton Street figure. The Vine almost reached to the corner of Southall's Lane but two more shops were squeezed onto the corner. One shop was occupied at one time by Frank Rider's sewing machine shop (no.44) and the corner shop itself was Emery's butchers shop (no.45). No.44 was occupied for a time by William Blewitt, the bookseller who had originally been on the other side of the road, and several people have tried to maintain the services of a butchers shop at no. 45 right up until recent times.

Southall's Lane has a history of its own which will be described briefly elsewhere but on the out-of-town corner was once the fairly imposing premises of The Duke of Wellington public house - a Hanson's pub associated with a landlord called Bert Austin. Beyond the pub were high three-storey houses which appear to have had courts built behind them - creating quite a densely populated area in Victorian times. The courts were probably demolished when the area was cleared to provide a location for North Worcestershire Motors who fronted onto Stafford Street.

Then came Chapel Street - so called because the

Ebenezer Chapel was built two thirds of the way up the street. This was the original home of the New Connexion Methodists - until they joined with the renegade Wesleyans from along Wolverhampton Street. It can still be seen on 1900 maps so it is not clear what happened to it in later years, and interestingly it is also marked on Treasure's map of the 1830s.

Crossing Chapel Street one came to Herbert Bayes' mineral waters factory at 55 Wolverhampton Street. There were more courts behind the factory, apparently accessed from Chapel Street. The triangle between Wolverhampton Street, Southall's Lane and Stafford Street, which included the world of Chapel Street was typical of the Victorian expansion of working class Dudley that extended down into "The Dock" - associated with Wellington Road and Stafford Street; making quite a contrast with the much more spacious and elegant Georgian expansion of Dudley found closer to the centre.

A few doors from Bayes' mineral waters factory were Pioli's ice-cream factory followed by Caddick's butchers shop and Foster's scrap merchants, and haulage contractors. At no.64 we came to the West End public house, where a well-known landlord had been George Collett, and his wife Lucy. Behind The West End was a blacksmith named Frank Powers who was a member of the Salvation Army. He was rather surrounded by pubs because The Hammer in Stafford Street must have backed onto his yard.

Left: The Vine Inn on the corner of Tinchbourne Street and Wolverhampton Street, in July 1979.
It has recently been a curry house but is currently empty. Tinchbourne Street itself provided access to the Sunday School building associated with the Methodist Chapel in Wolverhampton Street.
(Keith Hodgkins)

ESTABLISHED OVER FIFTY YEARS.

A. M. DUDLEY

(LATE PREECE & SON)

BOROUGH CARRIAGE WORKS,

43, Wolverhampton St., Dudley.

Broughams, Landaus,
Victorias,
Wagonettes,
Stanhope and
Mail Phaetons,
for Home & Exportation.

Coach and Carriage Builder

Estimates given and
Repairs done on the
shortest notice. . . .

Wagonettes

and other Vehicles for
Pleasure Parties, &c.

Sole Inventors and Patentees of the Patent

Stop & Drop Hinge for Dog Carts, &c.

Behind "The Vine", in premises described as 43 Wolverhampton Street, was The Borough Carriage Works - at one time owned by Preece & Son, then taken over by A.M.Dudley. The advertisement dates from 1905.

Above: George William Blewitt, photographed in 1939 when he married Catherine. George worked as a draughtsman in Sunderland during the War but in 1949 Catherine obtained a post as a librarian at Dudley Training College and George joined her with the intention of fulfilling a dream of opening a bookshop. He opened his bookshop at 157 Wolverhampton Street in 1952 and stayed there until moving across the road to no. 44. He died on 9th March 1985, and Catherine, who had later become a teacher at the Girls' Grammar School, carried on the business until 1990. (Francisca Wassell)

Right: The town-centre side of the junction of Wolverhampton Street and Southall's Lane, in April 1988. No.44 was then being used as Blewitt's Bookshop. After the bookshop closed in 1990 it became a video shop, and has since been empty.
No. 45, right on the corner has been used by various butchers. Just to the right, in Southall's Lane, are the premises where Billy Dainty was born. (NW).

Left: The Duke of Wellington stood on the out-of-town side of the junction of Wolverhampton Street and Southall's Lane, as photographed in July 1979. The building, with its distinctive corner, still exists and is currently used as "The Fireplace Warehouse". The three-storey buildings beyond still stand, 47 and 48 having become a fish and chip shop and 49 has become a graphic design business. The gap from there to Charlton Street, as Chapel Street is now called, has now been filled with small apartments.
(Keith Hodgkins)

Above: Chapel Street (now Charlton Street) is seen coming in on the left of this view of Wolverhampton Street looking towards Eve Hill in August 1964. Immediately beyond the junction was Bayes Mineral Water Factory, followed by 55 and 56 Wolverhampton Street.
(Graham Sidwell)

On the right hand side of Wolverhampton Street we can see the many little shops stretching from the Belper down to Dudley Factors at No.145. This distinctive building is seen on page 26 as Anyon's lamp oil shop.
The frequency of the no. 58 trollleybus service from Wolverhampton is self-evident. Trolleys 454 and 444 enter a narrow stretch of the street.

Right: The boarded-up windows of 57 Wolverhampton Street disfigure the premises once used to make Pioli's ice-cream, seen here in the 1980s. (Eric Bytheway)

Right: This wonderful building still stood on the corner of School Street and Wolverhampton Street in August 2005, but has since been demolished, despite its quality brickwork and distinctiveness. It was last used as offices by Westfield Stampings.
Note the cellar door on the side of the building - this was used as an air-raid shelter during the last War.
(NW)

On the far side of the Stafford Street/Wolverhampton Street junction was Eve Hill House and its gardens - still to be seen on the 1900 map reproduced by Alan Godfrey. This site would be recalled by most readers as the location of the Midland Counties Dairy's depot. The Dairy provided a 1930s semi art-deco contribution to the varied architecture of Wolverhampton Street with its distinctive tiling. To have the entrance to the depot right on a busy road junction made less and less sense as time went on but it seems to have been perpetuated in the entrance that now exists to a yard surrounded by industrial units.

The dairy abutted onto no. 65 (at one time 69) Wolverhampton Street which was the home of

Frank Preece, followed by a terrace of five houses, an entry and another pair. These survive today. But on reaching the corner of School Street we find an interesting building has been demolished. This was an attractive red-brick building which once provided warehousing and offices for Davenport's bottled beer. They moved to the other side of Wolverhampton Street, as described above, and the red-brick building was then used by GHL industrial painters. More recently it became the offices of Westfield Stampings - then it was suddenly "gone" - a classic example of that Black Country phenomenon: now you see it, now you don't! On the opposite corner were the premises of Messrs Lamsdale & Lewis, wholesale clothing manufacturers.

Beyond the clothing factory was a row of small cottages laying well back from the road on rising ground. These disappeared to make way for a petrol station, currently part of the Total group. A wall still runs from the petrol station up to the corner of Grange Road. This was the wall of Jesson's Junior School, now the modern Church of England primary school but once a charity school occupying The Shrubbery - a house that is clearly marked on Treasure's 1830s map. Wolverhampton Street stops at the junction with Grange Road leaving the Grange public house marooned on a site which was presumably thought-of as the top of Himley Road. This is the summit of Eve Hill, and one passes St. James' Church to progress into Salop Street.

Below:Fire engines turn out to a fire at the top of Wolverhampton Street about 1970. On the left is "Ye Old Struggling Man" and on the right, one of the Wolverhampton Corporation buses on the 58 route, replacing the former trolley buses from March 1967 onwards, passes the National Benzole filling station. The wall on the extreme right was the wall built in front of Jesson's School - my jumping off point in considering some of the features of the world that surrounded Eve Hill. (Paul Roberts)

Foot of page: Wolverhampton Corporation trolleybus no. 452 on the 58 route reaches the Eve Hill island and the Grange public house, on 18th February 1967. Note that Gorton's rope works still proudly advertises itself on the left and the spire of Top Church pops up in the background. (Graham Sidwell)

Chapter 3

More About Wolverhampton Street
A Tale of Two Agents

My discovery and rediscovery of Wolverhampton Street has unfolded over forty years or more. As an eighteen-year-old student making his way from the Training College into town and back in the early sixties there was one kind of experience. Twenty years later in the 1980s there was another kind of experience as a forty-year-old local historian delving into the history of Black Country institutions such as "shops". Another twenty years brings me into the twenty first century and a walk down Wolverhampton Street is yet another kind of experience, in which I can feel overwhelmed by the way in which things have changed or simply vanished. As someone who has always loved to collect information and record it, I feel all those lost opportunities to do more of such activities in the past has resulted in "gaps in the record" as well as physical gaps in the townscape.

Even in the devastated landscape of Wolverhampton Street today there are still two newsagents working away in the same locations used in the 1960s. Mr. Khan is still busy selling papers in the premises once used by the Bytheway family at no.150 and John and Cynthia Burgin are still selling papers at No. 167. While this book is being assembled in the summer of 2008, the Burgin

Family are celebrating the 140th anniversary of the business. For that reason let's look at "Burgin News" first.

Burgin News:
167 Wolverhampton Street.

The current business was established in January 1868 when John Burgin, once a carpet weaver from the Kidderminster area, decided that there was money to be made from the sale of newspapers, although at first books and stationery were also on sale. John added printing to the services he offered from 1881 onwards. The building - which also consists of the two shops next door - is thought to have been built in 1795. It was probably built for domestic use but by the 1850s was converted to shops. For many years the building belonged to the Hayden family who sold fish, but after the First World War it was bought by the Burgins.

John Burgin married twice and eventually had eight children. The youngest; Alfred, born in 1880, was destined to take over the business. On the eve of the First World War he took over when his mother, Mary Jane, died. However, Alfred then joined the

John and Cynthia Burgin in their Paper Shop at 167 Wolverhampton Street early in 2008, the third egenration of Burgins to be there. They are still at work in the shop as this book goes to press - assisted by members of the next two generations. Despite a few attacks and robberies, and changing conditions in the trade, it still seems that their policy is that customers should leave the shop with a smile on their face.
(NW)

Left: Burgin's Shop at 167 Wolver-hampton street in about 1905. Mary Jane Burgin (nee Hickman) stands in the doorway with her son Alfred. Mary Jane had married the original John Burgin in 1873 - on Christmas Day - so that no trade was lost at the shop! On becoming a widow she ran the business until 1914.
(Note that even when this picture qwas taken the shop was keen to advertise the length of time it had been in business.)
Alfred Burgin became the father of John Burgin, father and son both being born in the same room "on the premises". Alfred did not encourage John to become a newsagent and thus John originally went to the CWS "National Works" where he started to learn to be an electrician. when Alfred died his wife, Jane, took over - as in the previous generation and John and Cynthia therefore did not take over until Jane's death in 1978.

Left: The Burgin Family regard this as their second shopfront at 167 Wolverhampton Street, but in many respects it is simply a slight modification of the earlier one! This picture shortly after 1965 when the school next door was demolished and the site had become a car park. The door to the left is the entrance to John Burgin's "other" business as an electrical egineer.
(Both pictures are from the Burgin Family Collection)

services and had to leave the shop in the hands of his brother Harry. When Alfred returned he married Jane Willetts and resumed work at 167 Wolverhampton Street.

Alf and Jane had two children: Joan born in 1920 and John born in 1927. Alfred later told his son John that there would be no future in the business and encouraged John to pursue a career as an electrical engineer. Alf, who at one time was Chairman of the local Newsagents Federation, died in 1951 at the age of 71 and left his widow and daughter to carry on the business. It is a joke in the Burgin family that no-one has ever retired from the shop! Each generation has helped the previous one and eventually taken-over. Thus it was that when Jane died in 1978, John and Cynthia took over even though John was still involved in his own career. Today John and Cynthia are helped by daughter Susan and the grandchildren - the fifth generation of Burgins to be seen in the shop. They claim to be the oldest newsagency run by one family in the Midlands.

The Bytheways: 150 Wolverhampton Street.

George Bytheway trained as a hairdresser and at the age of seventeen opened a shop at the top of Himley Road. He was advised to try and obtain premises nearer the town centre and at some stage managed to move to 150 Wolverhampton Street. (The commencement of the business is usually quoted as 1892, but is not clear as to whether this refers to the date of opening in Himley Road, or the arrival in Wolverhampton Street.) Ironically, the male tradition of going to the barber's shop to be shaved began to die off after the First World War and George had to diversify. He originally purchased newspapers from Burgin's with the hope of passing them on to customers who came in for a shave or a haircut, but somehow this changed into the business of selling papers in their own right. George was also able to make umbrellas, and his shop window indicates that he also sold books, sweets and cigarettes.

Right: Bytheway's Shop can also be seen on page 29 - as it was in 1937. Here - in the post-war years - it is noticeable that the left hand side of the shop has returned to domestic use. Donald, seen on the left, took over the business from his mother just after the war, and married Violet in 1947 - bringing her into the business.
They ran the buisness at 150 Wolverhampton Street until the 1980s.

Right: Violet Bytheway at the counter at 150 Wolverhampton Street. Violet was normally to be found at the counter while Donald was 'out and about', and seemed to have retailing in her blood. Her mother had once run a little shop at Queens Cross, and before the War Violet had worked at Henry Wood's Grocery shop at 46 High Street.
(All photographs from Eric Bytheway's Collection)

A wonderful portrait of George Bytheway (1873- 1964) - one time hairdresser, umbrella manufacturer and newsagent and tobacconist of 150 Wolverhampton Street. George and his wife Elizabeth (1874 - 1944) are listed in the 1901 Census at this address, and George's occupation is listed as "hairdesser". Although he became a news agent by default, he took to the trade and became Secretary of the Dudley Branch of the National Federation of News Agents.He found it difficult to "retire"and continued to supervise long after his son Donald, and daughter-in-law Violet, were running the shop. In the end a road accident outside the shop in 1963 forced his retirement. George and Elizabeth had always been inventive when it came to increasing the range of services provided by the shop and at one time grew flowers and vegatables on an allotment at the bottom of Grange Road to sell in the shop. George was also an active member of the congregation of the Park Chapel, Grange Road.

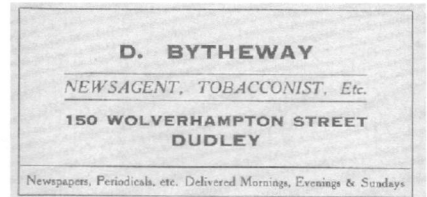

D. BYTHEWAY

NEWSAGENT, TOBACCONIST, Etc.

**150 WOLVERHAMPTON STREET
DUDLEY**

Newspapers, Periodicals, etc. Delivered Mornings, Evenings & Sundays

In the early days George had to collect the papers early in the morning from Dudley Station, but in the 1920s newspaper wholesalers became established in Dudley. George also eventually became secretary of the Newsagents Federation, working alongside Alf Burgin.

George's son, Donald, was born in 1917 and he took over the business in the 1940s having already worked in the shop since leaving school in the previous decade. Donald married Violet in 1947 and as usual in this business Violet was often to be seen behind the counter. It was Violet's illness in 1983 that led Donald to retire and sell the business. During the fifty years that Donald had been involved in the newspaper trade he felt he had seen it decline from being a real trade to simply being a sideline - alongside selling just about everything else! Donald's immediate successor lasted barely a year in the business but since then the store has been run by Mr. Khan.

The pub next door: The Fox Inn

Bytheways shop was next door to the Fox Inn - more than just another of Wolverhampton Street's many pubs as, although it closed in 1946, its bar still survives today, because it has been preserved and installed in the Bottle & Glass public house in the Black Country Living Musuem!

Like many of the buildings along Wolverhampton Street, The Fox was probably older than we might have expected. Joe Wade claimed the building was erected in 1726. Joe was born in 1874 and it is not clear when he first became licensee of The Fox, but it may have been as early as 1902. Don Bytheway could remember Joe in the 1930s when he served behind the bar dressed in a billy-cock hat, white apron, and bright check shirt. His bar was decorated with stuffed animal heads, antlers and horns, and all kinds of curios. Joe ran his pub along strict lines.

Above: Donald Bytheway with some of his models and clock - all built by Donald except for the Bassett Lowke "Mogul" standing on the box. Right: Donald's son Eric races past the Fox Inn several years after it had closed. (Bytheway Collection)

There was a sign behind the bar saying, "Avoid nasty language and do not drink too much or you will give Joe Wade the chance of telling you the tap has been stopped". Another local legend tells how Joe Wade would only allow Friday night customers one drink if they were on their way home from work as he wanted to make sure some of the pay-packet reached home!

After the pub closed in 1946, Joe Wade's daughter, Josephine, continued to look after the bar. Joe Wade died in 1950 and Josephine was even more resolved to make sure the bar survived. She was secretary of Dudley's History & Archaeological Society, and her connections made it possible to persuade Richard Traves, Dudley's Keeper of Science and Archaeology, to move the bar to Dudley Art Gallery and Musuem in St. James's Road in 1974. Eventually it moved to the Black Country Living Museum in the 1980s.

Top: a panoramic view of Dudley Teacher Training Collge when new, as seen from the sports field. The sports field survives but this building has now been demolished.

Centre: College Hall, or "North Hall" as it was originally called. It matched the main college building and survived until Wolverhampton University sold the land for redevelopment. This picture was taken on 8th June 2002 at the "Final Farewell" event.

Left: St. George's Hall, King Edmund Street, opened in the Autumn of 1962. This was my first home in Dudley.

St. Mary's and St. George's later beceme known as Worcester and Stafford Halls.

(NW and Lilian Sheldon)

Chapter 4
What's In Front of Eve Hill?

The late Victorian regular street pattern of Eve Hill that created St. James's Terrace and the other streets to the west of Salop Street, was mirrored on the eastern side of Eve Hill by the creation of King Edmund Street and Castle View. In the 1900s The Parade provided access to the Vicarage and grave-yard at the back of St. James' church and to King Edmund Street but then halted. The houses in these two streets were not very grand but they afforded good views across open fields, then known as Priory Fields.

These fields became the location of Dudley Teacher Training College: a local response to the national shortage of teachers at the turn of the century, itself a result of the effects of the introduction of univer-sal educational provision beginning to be felt. The foundation stone of the new college was laid on 10th September 1908, by the Countess of Dudley. Local builders, Messrs Oakley & Coulson, began construction of the buildings designed by Birmingham architects, Crouch, Butler & Savage, and the official opening was able to take place the following year.

National Government paid 75% of the costs, but apart from that the project was supported by the Worcestershire and Staffordshire authorities. The college was opened by the Minister of Education, Walter Runciman MP, on 16th July 1909. Almost immediately work began on enlarging the college!

The college originally provided places for about 10 students, most of whom would have lived locally. Hostel accommodation was provided for female students - fifty in the North Hostel (later called "College Hall") and about half that number at The Mount in Dixon's Green on the opposite side of town. After the Second World War additional hostel accommodation was provided at "Lingwood" in St. James's Road, and later in modern purpose built premises at "Broadway Hall". Further halls fol-lowed in buildings along St. James's Road, the only such building still in existence being "Eversleigh".

Teacher Education went through a number of changes over the years and I arrived in Dudley just as the old two-year training was being replaced by a three-year programme. This change entailed mas-sive enlargement of staff and facilities. I arrived just in time to help put furniture into the brand new halls of residence built in King Edmund Street and to use the brand new teaching facilities, officially opened on 21st November 1962 by Princess Margaret and Lord Snowdon. I only remember trivial details of this event suggesting that I had not yet developed a sense of history!

The college had a campus that was "old and new" and that polarity extended to almost every aspect of college life - one foot in the past, one foot in the present. Perhaps that was a feature of life in the early 1960s in all walks of life, and because of the risk of doubling the size of this book, I will not explore the strange world of Dudley Training College very much further! In 1962 it was impossi-ble to foresee that one day the campus would sim-ply become an outpost of a university based in Wolverhampton, and when that happened it was impossible to imagine that the university would eventually abandon the site.

Because I have been blessed with a life full of inter-esting twists and turns, I found myself teaching for one year (1981/82) for Wolverhampton University in the very rooms where I had been "teacher-trained" twenty years earlier. In 2007 I returned once again and taught in a room which had become the property of Dudley Technical College. Meanwhile on 8th June 2002 I had attended a "final farewell and reunion" event which was seen as the closure of the campus. On top of all this it seems strange to see what parts of the college survive in 2008, and what has disappeared. Even more diffi-cult to work out is what impact did this institution have on its host community? Instead of celebrating its centenary in 2009, we will be wondering, "What ever became of Dudley Training College?"

Left: Princess Margaret opens the new facilities at Dudley Training College on 21st November 1962. From then on it became "Dudley College of Education." She is watched by Lord Snowdon on the right and the college Principal, David Jordan, on the left. (NW Collection)

Centre: The caretaker's lodge at the Teacher Training College, Castle View entrance, on 8th June 2002. The main college building in the background has now been replaced with a modern housing development and Castle View is "blocked-off" at this point. At present the lodge remains in place, the last remnant of the 1909 campus. (NW)

Below: About forty four years separate these pictures of the steps in front of St. Mary's Hall. An unidentified student of 1964 vintage on the left. A "reunion group" at the same location on 5th July 2007 on the right (NW)

Above: On Saturday 8th June 2002 a hastily organised event took place to allow ex-students to say "Farewell" to the campus that had once been their "Training College", "College of Education", or "Faculty of Wolverhampton University" (depending on your age group!). Mr. White delivered a 'Farewell Address' in the Main Hall and people gathered for a fairly informal group photograph outside. Ironically the buildings seen here have survived and the ones behind the camera have beendemolished! (NW)

Below: A high angle view across the College of Education complex at Eve Hill, probably taken from one of the Eve Hill flats. St. George's and St. Mary's Halls are seen in the foreground with their ground floor connecting buildings which housed lounges and a canteen. Beyond are the older original buildings of the college, then we see the slopes of the Wren's Nest rising from the surrounding housing estate. In the distance, the Black Country extends away to the east. Picture taken in 1981. (Express & Star)

Above: Looking down Park Road, now Parkway Road, Eve Hill, with Park View on the left (the home of Josiah Lane). On the right is the old malthouse, followed by Josisah Lane's glassworks, although no longer in use as such when this picture was taken in 1959. (Dudley Archives & Local History Centre)

Below: The wedding of Alfred Lane, chief clerk in his father's glassworks and Mabel Harper on Easter Monday 20th April 1914. Josiah and Amelia Lane are 3rd and 4th from left on the seated row. The Harpers, of Waddams Pool Ironworks, are on the right of the couple. Having married at St. James' Church they have assembled in the glassworks yard for the photo! Many other "links by marriage" are represented here. Eg. Gertrude Lane who married John Whitmore (Fruit & Poultry retailer) is just behind the bride, and Lucy Lane who married Arthur Griffiths - of Jesson's School connection! (See page 53) (Molly James' Collection)

Chapter 5
What's Behind Eve Hill?

If you pass through a Black Country town, by car or public transport, you can become acquainted with the main arteries - usually named after their eventual destination with wonderful symmetry, so, for example Wolverhampton Street, Dudley, will eventually take you to Dudley Street, Wolverhampton. However, there are always more worlds to discover on either side of these arteries. Thus, when it comes to exploring Dudley, it is often a matter of seeing what is "behind" or "in front" of the world first encountered.

I got to know Eve Hill by trudging up and down Salop Street and Wolverhampton Street, but there has always been another world just around and beyond Eve Hill. Exploring this world today I would start at the Park Congregational Church at the foot of Grange Road, and would head out across Grange Park until reaching Himley Road. I would then ascend Occupation Street to reach Windmill Drive just behind Butterfield Court - the sole survivor of Eve Hill's famous tower-block flats. Passing through a kissing gate in Windmill Drive, it is possible to come across Dudley's vanished football pitch and then take in a view of Shaver's End from behind the Struggling Man pub. Shaver's End is Dudley's NW Frontier and has several interesting features, as we will see.

It is also possible to take a tighter circle around the back of Salop Street. We could begin at the site of Jesson's School at the top of Wolverhampton Street, make our way along Park Road, now Parkway Road and reach Himley Road almost opposite Occupation Street. From the top of Himley Road, we could take in the narrow streets around St. James's Terrace, now lost - not beneath the tower-blocks of the 1960s - but beneath the modern redevelopment that has replaced the tower-blocks! Once again this would take us to Shaver's End.

Let's look at some of the locations of interest in a combination of these routes. Jesson's School had an address as 88 Wolverhampton Street, and some folk referred to it simply as "No.88", perhaps meaning the schoolmaster's house. From 1913 to 1946 this was inhabited by Arthur Edgar Griffiths, the Headmaster, and his wife Lucy who was another of the daughters of Josiah Lane of the Eve Hill Glassworks. Arthur and Lucy had five children, three of which became teachers. Their son Ted, for example, is still alive at the time of writing and had a teaching career that went from working at Netherton's C.of E. school to being Headteacher at St. John's, Kates Hill. Arthur's mother, Thirza Griffiths, was Headmistress at St. James' School, Eve Hill, and it is her name that is now immor-

Right: "Park Villa" at 74 Grange Road, as it is today. This was the home of Josiah Lane, proprietor of the Eve Hill Glassworks. Grange Road goes to the left of this picture and on the right we look down Park Road (now Parkway Road) towards the one-time home of Dorothy Round, Dudley's famous tennis champion. (NW)

Two contemporary views from Butterfield Court, the last remaining tower block on Eve Hill. Above: This view looks down on Occupation Street as it meets the top of Windmill Street, and Whitehall Drive descending into London Heights. To the left Grange Park is visible, and one looks across the Russell's Hall Estate to Brierley Hill, the Russell's Hall Hospital and beyond... (NW)

Below: In the foreground of this view is part of the Shaver's End football pitch, once home to Dudley Football team. London Fields is on the left, then comes the Dibdale Road making its way towards Gornal, and on the extreme right is the lower end of Fairview Road. This whole area was intensively mined during the nineteenth century. (NW)

talised on the board outside the school building in the Black Country Museum!

Jesson's School had an interesting history stretching back to the 1850s. John William Jesson left provisions in his will of 1855 to pay for the education and clothing of 7-14 year old boys. The school was created in a former house called "The Shrubbery", but I am not sure whether this had once been John Jesson's home. It catered for about forty boys who also had to attend services at St. James' Church. At some later stage it became a mixed infants school but remained very small - possibly only having four classrooms. The modern primary school on the site was opened in 1996.

Just beyond Jesson's School is the junction of Grange Road and Wolverhampton Street as it reaches Eve Hill. The houses of Grange Road still embody some past splendour, on the left are elegant terraces of the 1890s and on the right are large semi-detached houses commanding dramatic rear views across Grange Park. This must have been a leafy suburb of the 1890s, when the park was new. Grange Park occupies land that had once been New Town Colliery. In about 1892 the waste-land of old pit-banks was purchased by Dudley Council and was landscaped to create a recreation ground. (Similar projects helped create Buffery Park, Woodside Park and Netherton Park.) The large semis of Grange Road really backed on to an extension of the recreation ground that turned it into the park we would recognise today. At the top of Grange Road is Park Villa - once the home of Josiah Lane, proprietor of the Eve Hill Glassworks.

Descendents of the Lane family have researched the history of "Dudley's last glassworks" and trace the story back to Thomas Lane and his son, Josiah Lane Snr., born in 1837. The family established a glassworks in Hampton Street, Birmingham in 1865. The story moves to Dudley in about 1888 when Josiah, and his son, another Josiah, establish a glassworks in Park Road, Eve Hill. It may have been a new enterprise or an existing glassworks they had taken-over.

Josiah Lane Jnr. moved into 48 Wellington Road, but later moved to Park Villa at the top of Grange Road. The house still exists today, although the glassworks around the corner in Park Road has been demolished, along with the adjacent malthouse. Josiah entered the civic life of Dudley on becoming a councillor in November 1906, as well as serving as church warden at St. James Church, Eve Hill for twenty years. He died of a heart attack on 8th September 1932. It then became clear that he had kept his glassworks going, although it was losing money, to save the jobs of his employees. Inevitably the glassworks closed at the end of 1932. Josiah, his wife Amelia and daughter Kate, are buried in a fairly prominent grave in St. James' churchyard.

Parkway Road, as Park Road is now called, still bears traces of the malthouse and glassworks, as well as being home to the present-day Quaker Meeting House, and to a factory where "Dave's Baltis" are made. The most famous resident of Park Road was Dorothy Round from no.11.

The junction of Parkway Road with Himley Road is almost opposite the entrance of Occupation Street - the last survivor of a network of streets around St. James's Terrace, and the streets that ran up to Salop Street: West Street, Dudley Street, Peel Street and Windmill Street. These streets, and King Edmund Street running parallel to the other side of Salop Street, formed the "village" of Eve Hill - a mid to late nineteenth century "suburb" of Dudley where poor colliers and nailers lived alongside some better-off neighbours. (It is shown as an already very densely built-up area on the 1883 "Union" maps of Dudley.) While at Dudley College of Education from 1962 to 1965, I watched the clearing and demolition of these streets - thinking that the replacement flats would last forever. (Wrong again!)

Although many houses in Occupation Street have been modernised, it is worth visiting to capture the feel of "old" Eve Hill. Pause at no.58 to think that this was once the home of Anne Brown - once an Anglican at St. James' Church, but saved and converted to Pentacostalism at the Jeffreys Crusade at Dudley Town Hall in 1930. She later built her own "temple" near Woods Lane, Quarry Bank.

The top of Occupation Street joins Windmill Drive just behind Butterfield Court. Treasure's map of Dudley of 1835 records the location of the windmill on this site. Today this windy position provides views westward across the Russells Hall Estate, and across the modern housing found at London Heights

- presumably a modern re-working of the name London Fields where some nineteenth century streets cluster around the narrow crossroads of Corser Street and Dibdale Street. Around London Fields had once been small pits and a hearth furniture works.

Just before coming to Dudley's northern boundary the present-day explorer comes across an amazing discovery - the remains of a football pitch. This was once the home of Dudley Football Club, before they moved to land adjacent to the Cricket Ground near Birmingham Road in 1913. They once played in their black and white "strip" on this Shaver's End pitch, with its terraced sides. The teams changed in the Struggling Man, on the corner of Dibdale Road. The chairman of the club was none other than Josiah Lane of the Eve Hill Glassworks, better known for his support of Birchfield Harriers. The pitch was later used by The Phoenix Football Club, but looking at it today it is difficult to imagine that it was ever level enough on which to play football.

From the Struggling Man one gazes into the hamlet of Shaver's End where there was once a toll gate on the road to Sedgley. On Treasure's Map of 1835 the whole of what became Salop Street is shown as "Shaver's End", but today we apply that name, if we have encountered it at all, to the stretch of road now called Highland Road. Cottages dating from the 1860s and 1870s still occupy one side of this road. Beyond the cottages is the Shavers End Reservoir - just across the boundary into the one-time Urban District of Sedgley. The reservoir was developed by the South Staffordshire Waterworks Company to provide a store and head of water from which to supply Dudley. Their water came from wells in the Lichfield area along an aqueduct put beneath the tracks of the South Staffordshire Railway, to a "terminal" at Park Lane, Tipton. From there the water had to be pumped up to Shaver's End.

The reservoir was not the only item of interest just over the boundary in Sedgley. The most obvious centre of interest was the Dudley Workhouse building which eventually became the Burton Road Hospital - on a site now occupied by modern housing. The Dudley Poor Law Union was set up in 1834 as a result of the Poor Law Amendment Act and the "union" consisted of the parishes of Dudley, Sedgley, Coseley and Rowley Regis. Their new workhouse was ready for use by 1859 - replacing former workhouses in the centres of Dudley and Sedgley. At the beginning of the 20th Century it also began to be used as a hospital and was enlarged for that purpose. Later the Rosemary Ednam Maternity Hospital was added. Whenever I passed the building on my trips of the 1960s on the No.58 trolleybuses I was reminded of grim legends I had heard of wards occupied by people institutionalised for strange out-dated reasons. Many Black Country hospital sites never quite threw off their past association with the world of the workhouse. As soon as the hospital was demolished in 1994 I wondered why I had never photographed it!

The "Dudley Houses" are six semi-detached houses of 1911 vintage built in Fairview Road, for the "Respectable Poor". The foundation stone was laid on 24th May 1911 by the Mayoress, Mrs. Bean. (NW)

Less noticeable than the Burton Road Hospital is a small row of six semi-detached houses in Fairview Road. These are the six "Dudley Houses". They were built in 1911 by Messrs. Oakley & Coulson of Stafford Street, for the Reginald Unwin Dudley Charity. They were built to house "the respectable poor" but it is not clear what kind of test the poor were put to in order to assess their respectability.

Above:The Burton Road Hospital complex seen from the air, not long before closure in 1993. Dibdale Road is in the foreground, where we see the buildings of the Castle Meadows Nursing Home. Behind them are the single storey hutment buildings of the 'C' wards with the 'OT' department to the right. Far right are the buildings of the Rosemary Ednam Maternity Ward and the Nurses Home. Most wards in the hospital provided accommodation for elderly people with mental health problems. (Cynthia Ho)

Burton Road Hospital began life as a 'workhouse' planned by the Board of Guardians of a Poor Law Union that took in the former parishes of Dudley, Sedgley and Rowley Regis. Planning began in 1856 and it was completed to the stage where it could take in the first inmates in the summer of 1859. It was enlarged and modified over the years particularly on becoming a hospital in the twentieth century.

Right: The main entrance to the Burton Road complex seen from the gardens that separated it from the main road.
(Collection of Kim Elwell)

Right: Burton Road Hospital closed in December 1993 and remaining patients were transferred to new facilities at Bushey Fields. This picture was taken in 1993 as the hospital closed down. The X-Ray and Chest Clinic seen here may have already closed by then. Demolition followed closure and modern housing now fills most of the site.
(Cynthia Ho)

Right: A telephoto picture taken from the top of Butterfield Court about 1980 shows the rambling nature of the Burton Road Hospital site, in which nineteenth century buildings have been supplemented with hut-like buildings. (Legend has it that US soldiers were billeted here during the Second World War.)
Beyond the hospital is open ground stretching away to the Dormston Trading Estate built on former colliery tips, and the top of Jews Lane.
(Express & Star)

Chapter 6
What's In Front of Top Church?

Top Church is the Black Country's Eiffel Tower. Its spire can not only be seen from many parts of Dudley, but can also be spotted from many other vantage points in the region. From even further afield the spire can be glimpsed once you are trained to recognise it. In one of my early trips around the area, Jack Aldiss had told me that one of the key things I needed to know about Dudley was that Top Church was 'low church' and that Bottom Church was 'high church'. I absorbed this information and mentally noted their respective positions - St. Edmund's at the foot of Castle Hill, and St. Thomas' at the other end of the town's centre. Many years were to elapse before I ventured inside both churches!

Eventually I realised that Top church did more than mark the end of the main part of Dudley High Street, it also stood strategically between two interesting subdivisions of Dudley. Behind the church was the world of 'Flood Street' in which this one street seemed to give its name to the whole area, but what was in front of Top Church? I realised that I could reach Top Church, from my base in Eve Hill, not just via Wolverhampton Street and the High Street, but more directly via Stafford Street. Exploring Stafford Street was stimulated by Dudley Library's temporary removal to the one-time infant school building in that street, and by hearing fellow students' descriptions of their visits to the Gypsy's Tent.

Right: Top Church pops out from behind the Co-op building at the top of Dudley's High Street, although there are various other ways of approaching it. Its 175 foot high spire can be seen for miles and has recently been renovated.
St. Thomas' church became the parish church of Dudley in 1646 after St. Edmund's had become a victim of the Civil War. On 25th October 1816 Luke Booker, the Vicar of Dudley, laid the foundation stone of this building to replace the old church. An iron-framed building, faced in Bath stone was erected with a view to holding at least 1200 people. Over the years there have been many additions to the building and refurbishments - even a little shrapnel damage added in 1940. (NW)

The Gypsy's Tent stood at the junction of Stafford Street and Steppingstone Street. It is the descent of Steppingstone Street which revealed the secrets of what lay in front of Top Church. It was the gateway to "The Old Dock" - an intriguing maze of streets that underwent drastic "clearance" in the 1960s. Both Flood Street and the Old Dock had been areas of Dudley that grew rapidly in the nineteenth century, becoming densely populated and industrialised. 20th century Dudley had to deal with the legacy of these places, although at first it was not clear how the physical frontiers of Dudley could expand to find space to re-house its population. Acquiring the land on which to build the Priory Estate in the mid 1920s started the process of clearing Flood Street - a process which was almost completed by the 1960s, having been interrupted by the Second World War.

The entrance to Stafford Street is directly opposite the front of Top Church, seen here in 2007. The street is flanked by The Three Crowns pub (The "Brewery Tap" for Hanson's Brewery which is just behind it), on one side and a line of several buildings on the other which includes the frontage of the Regent cinema, later known as the Gaumont. (The auditorium is well back behind this frontage.)
Our journey round The Dock criss-crosses Stafford Street, this end of which is shown as Mill Street on Treasure's Map of 1835. (NW)

The area around Hanson's Brewery was being demolished when this picture was taken in April 1968. The bench on the right looks out over upper High Street from Greystone Street. The brewery was demolished in the early 1990s. (NW)

There were other areas of open space in and around Dudley but such areas were really vast tracts of industrial wasteland created and contaminated by early nineteenth century coal mining. These areas could not be used to alleviate Dudley's housing problems until they could be stabilised and cleaned-up. One such area was The Old Park, on which the present Russell's Hall Estate was eventually built. Urban Dudley expanded across Wellington Road from The Old Dock to The New Dock in the 1890s, but clearing The Old Dock could not get underway for another sixty years. During that time The New Dock formed a western frontier to Dudley and people living there could look out over open space. The nearest open space was turned into allotments and a nine-hole golf-course.

Treasure's Map of 1835 shows Dock Farm at the point where Steppingstone Street runs into Dock Lane. The latter proceeded to Wellington Road, probably laid down in the 1820s when such a street name was fashionable. Some rather grand houses were built on Wellington Road over the years, but the streets on either side were over-crowded and without amenities. In Dock Lane itself the "Model Dwellings" were built in 1854 to try and demonstrate reasonable standards of house-building but the rest of The Dock was a Victorian free-for-all that provided both very solidly built houses as well as slum-like "courts". Quite a stunning development was Victoria Terrace. When I first saw it I could not tell to what extent it was still inhabited and to what extent it had been cleared. It seemed to be sinking

Our boozy entry into The Old Dock continues!

Above left: A drawing of Julia Hanson & Sons' Brewery, with the spire of Top Church visible in the background. Julia's sons built this brewery in the 1890s. In 1943 it became part of Wolverhampton & Dudley Breweries Ltd.

Top right: The Windmill Inn, Stafford Street, built in 1830, and backing on to Hanson's Brewery! (Closed early 1950s.)

Centre: The Gypsy's Tent - home to Millard's Home-brewed Ales, photographed August 1968.
Steppingtone Street is on the right. (NW)

Right: The Oddfellows Arms of 1841, half way down Steppingstone Street, on the corner of Albert Street. (Photographed 1985) (NW)

into the ground to fool the advancing bull-dozers.

Evidence of the nineteenth century population explosion in The Dock was found in the response of the churches. A mission chapel was established on the corner of Charlotte Street and Dock Lane, only about a quarter of a mile from Top Church but in a different world! By the time I came across it in the mid sixties, it stood in glorious isolation and I paused to photograph it despite failing to photograph most of The Dock. Eventually St. Luke's was built in 1876, facing Wellington Road, and the area became a new parish. Ironically, the parishes have now been re-united and St. Luke's Church and the interim mission church have vanished completely.

The Congs and the Prims showed their usual enthusiasm for embracing the working classes and both were keen to build chapels in The Dock. The Prims, who had become established in the Flood Street area early on by building a chapel in George Street in 1829, eventually built a very substantial chapel on Wellington Road in 1861. It survived to become a Sikh temple, which has subsequently been rebuilt. The Congregationalists pushed through The Dock and on into The New Dock with missions that were eventually replaced with the 1906 building on the corner of Himley Street and Maughan Street. It was built with evangelistic enthusiasm combined with a strong sense of social purpose. It was described as an "institute" church and provided baths as well as

Above: A panoramic view of The Old Dock about 1963 just before clearance and wholesale demolition began. Dock Lane runs right through the centre of the picture, becoming Steppingstone Street as it reaches the

Oddfellow's Arms on the extreme right. Leading off Dock Lane is Oxford Street heading towards Stafford Street, and on the right Victoria Terrace shows up in all its magnitude. In the foreground we can see Charlotte Street making its way past the Co-operative Bucket & Fender Works, of which the roofs are visible. At the junction of Charlotte Street and Dock Lane stands the little chapel - seen from Charlotte Street in April 1968 in the picture on the left. (Dudley Archives & Local History Centre)

Left: The Dock Lane Mission. It seems obscure who first built this chapel but by the early 1870s it was used by the Church of England as a "mission" from St. Thomas' Church (ie:"Top Church"). Leadership was provided by the Church Army. It seems to have ceased being used as a place of worship in the 1930s, and for a time was used as a warehouse by the Dudley Furnishing Company. It was demolished about 1970. (NW)

The Metropolitan Association for Improving the Dwellings of the Industrial Classes built this row of "model" houses in Dock Lane in 1854, but apparently lacked funds or support for building others. The street on the right is Prince Albert Street, and in the distance is Ludgate Street. In the foreground is Earl Garner's off-licence. (Shiela Aston)

opportunities for spiritual guidance. It was led by key figures like Thomas Amos and A.T. Price. It has recently celebrated its centenary and is well worth visiting to become acquainted with the past and present world of The Dock.

Another interesting feature of The Dock was its industrialisation, paralleled by the industrialisation of the area between the town centre and Dixon's Green. At first I was fooled by the prosperous market-town "feel" of Dudley in the 1960s, and did not realise the mistake people made when they said that Dudley was the least industrialised of the Black Country towns. Such a view failed to take into account the nineteenth century history of Dudley and its legacy. When nineteenth century Dudley was not being plagued by its problems of water supply and poor local governance, it was faced with turmoil in the coal trade, decline of the nail trade and the loss of its glass industry. Opportunities to devel-

op industries were seized and out of this grew specialisations like bedstead and hearth ware manufacturing. Key Dudley public figures owned works in The Dock, like the Paragon Works in Angel Street (Thomas Adshead), and the Ivanhoe Works off Oxford Street (James Smellie). The Victoria Works was built right out on the New Dock frontier. All these can be clearly seen on the turn-of-the-century map reproduced by Alan Godfrey.

One of the most interesting works, from my point of view was the workers' co-operative created to establish the Dudley Co-operative Bucket and Fender Society. This commenced business in April 1888, and may have grown out of the failure of an earlier similar venture. By 1890 its President was Mark Round, a well-known Dudley figure. The secretary was Joseph Edwards who played a part in "saving" the Dudley Co-operative Society after its financial crisis of 1892. It would be wonderful to be able to

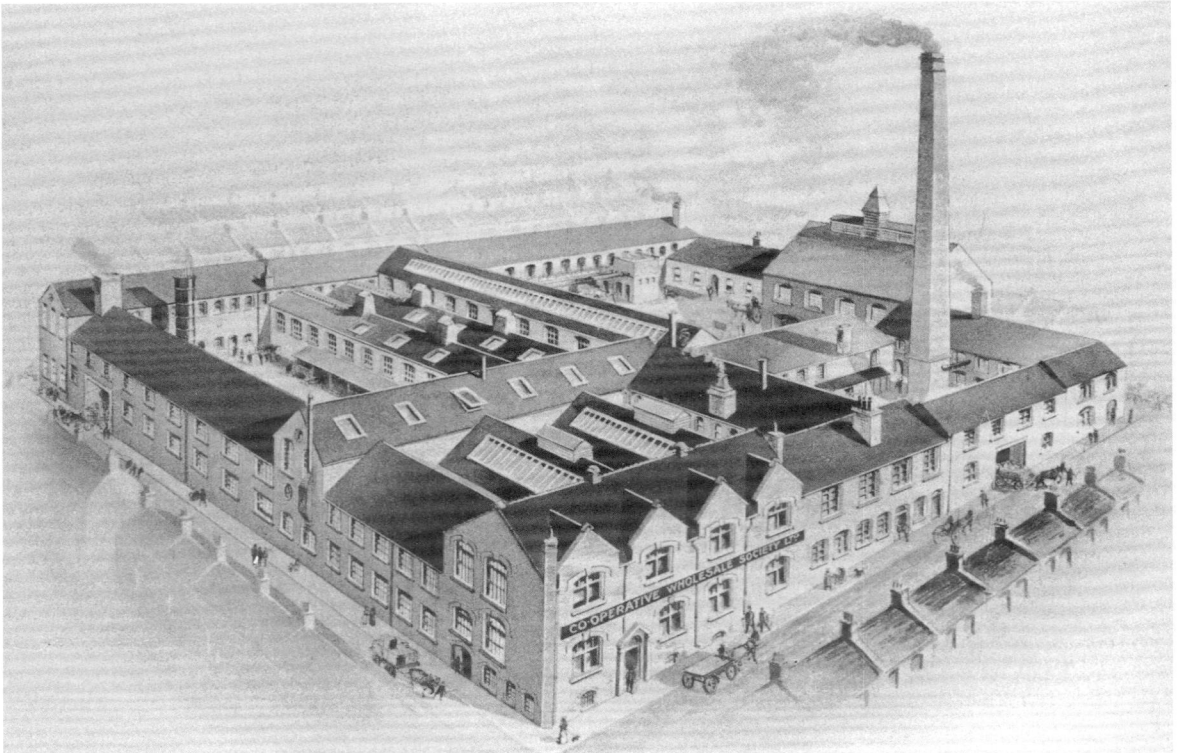

Above: The Dudley Co-operative Bucket & Fender Society's works as illustrated on their headed notepaper. In the foreground are the offices facing Charlotte Street, as seen in close-up below. (Co-op Collection)

Below: The gable-end seen on the extreme left of the above picture survives today although most of the works have vanished. The lettering suggests that the CWS modernised this part of the works in 1919. (NW)

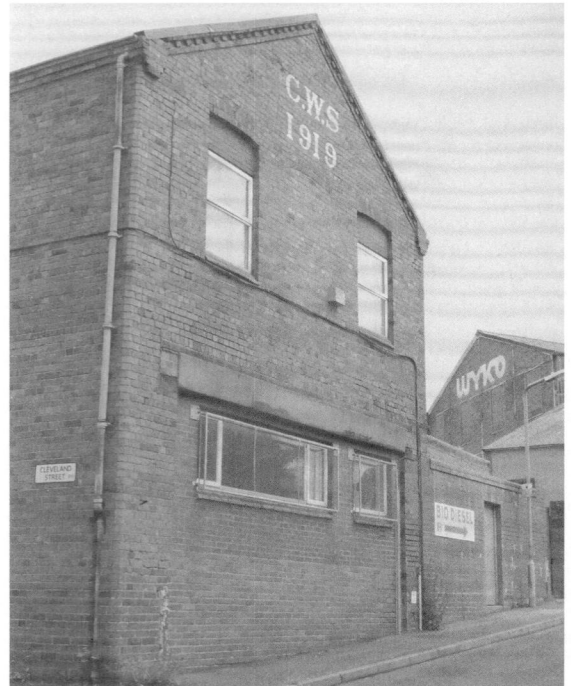

unravel the links that may have existed between the Bucket & Fender Society and the retail society.

The Bucket and Fender Society expanded in the 1890s and that is probably when the Charlotte Street Works took shape. Its galvanised products and hearth furniture were sold to many Co-operative Societies, but for some reason it was absorbed by the CWS (The Co-operative Wholesale Society) in 1908. Usually the CWS took this step when a local society was in trouble! The CWS stayed in The Dock until the mid 1930s when they transferred their operations to the National Works in Waddams Pool. (See subsequent chapter.)

Another interesting feature of The Dock was the landsale wharf established in 1865 when the Earl of Dudley's railway reached this point on the outskirts of town. The line had worked its way across the wastes of The Old Park - already exhausted by the second half of the nineteenth century - and was reached from The Wallows (the "hub" of the Earl's railway system) via the line that wandered between Low Town and Fens Pool, passed under 'Mantle's Bridge' and headed into The Old Park. The line and the wharf survived until the immediate post-war period, probably giving up at the time of the nationalisation of the coal industry.

As made clear earlier, the New Dock on the western side of Wellington Road was a real frontier settlement although the houses of Lawley Street and Maughan Street were probably not much better than those found in The Old Dock. These have been replaced in the 1960s but The Hearty Goodfellow still provides some Victorian "presence" to the area. During Victorian times Waterloo Road ran into a street carrying the wonderful name: "Thirteen House Row", but this was later renamed "St. Luke's Row."

While travelling back and forth between my flat in Pensnett Road, Holly Hall, and the college up at Eve Hill, I enjoyed a variety or routes. I could take Ashenhurst Road through the fringe of the new Russell's Hall Estate - then being built - and up to the Congregational Chapel and into Grange Road, or I could come via Wolverhampton Street, Stafford Street and Wellington Road. The latter route provided a better view of what was going on in The Dock, and the neighbouring areas.

Stafford Street began with the modern 1930s's tiled walls of the Midland Counties Dairy and next door was once the site of Price's Bakery. There seems to have been a profusion of bakeries in the area: Reynold's behind Wolverhampton Street, and Davies' and Rhodes' down Wellington Road. Small independent bakeries were in the process of disappearing by the early sixties to be replaced by larger modern plant owned by national combines, where the product emerged sliced and wrapped.

Wellington Road is shown clearly on Treasure's map of 1835 but traversed open fields on the outskirts of built-up Dudley at the time. Substantial houses were built in the road, plus two churches and by the beginning of the 20th century it had become the "boundary" between" The Old Dock and The New Dock. When people were rehoused from both areas in the 1960s some moved into the tower blocks seen here behind "Summerfield House". Four towers were built between 1964 and 1965 by Wimpey & Co. Picture taken in 2007. (NW)

Above: The Primitive Methodist Chapel in Wellington Road in its "rebuilt form" dating from 1869. (A chapel had been on the site since 1861.) It closed in 1961 and the congregation joined Central in Wolverhampton Street. The building became a Sikh gurdwara, and has since been completely rebuilt.
(Dudley Archives & Local History Centre)

Right: St. Luke's Church of England Church, built 1876, closed in 1967 and demolished in 1973. A postcard illustrates the interior (Ken Rock) *and the drawing of the exterior comes from a Blocksidge's Guide.*

The next building in Stafford Street had been Coulson's Joinery Works - a builder, building suppliers and joiners all rolled into one. It seems that the enterprise grew out of a Victorian family building concern called Nelson's (hence Nelson Road) and in later reincarnations the firm seems to have built a number of local buildings of note. What is interesting is that this building survives as a snooker club, but its previous use is still indicated by the wording in the gables. Behind this workshop are the twin streets: Edward Street and Alexandra Street and the streets that once surrounded the Park Schools: another little enclave.

The 'town side' of Stafford Street started with the back yard of The West End Hotel, followed by The

Hammer Inn, but in the days when I regularly traversed this area, it had been redeveloped by the North Worcestershire Garage Company. Today new housing has been built in the triangle between Chapel Street, Stafford Street and Southalls Lane, but remarkably the old King and Queen pub still stands on the corner, although it has now been converted to flats. On the opposite corner is The Shakespeare: the living embodiment of that slogan "unspoilt by progress"! If you came out of The Shakespeare, crossed Stafford Street and proceeded straight into Oxford Street you were led directly into the heart of The Dock. The entrance to Oxford Street is still there if you know where to look. The building between the crossroads and Oxford Street had once been a factory belonging to Messrs

Raybould & Whitehouse - industrial chemists and manufacturers of polish.

Southalls Lane, which has come up to the cross-roads from the left, also has its share of history - of little shops and houses that have disappeared and some that have survived. To modern car-drivers making their way into Dudley it must simply seem to be a short extension of Wellington Road. Car drivers ascending the upper part of Stafford Street today will only be aware of car parks, new health centres, and the Magistrates' Court. However, once upon a time, this outer face of The Dock was full of shops, some schools and, of course, more pubs such as The Five Ways Inn, on the corner of Inhedge. On the opposite side of Stafford Street is The Gypsy's Tent - which is more or less where we began our exploration of what lay in front of Top Church.

(For a more detailed tour of The Dock as it once was see John Stenson's book, "Gone But Not Forgotten", published by the author in 1999.)

Right: "Old Sol" furniture polish was made by Raybould Whitehouse & Co. in their chemical works on the corner of Stafford Street and Wellington Road where the Sandhar Supermarket is currently sited. Advert from a 1922 Unionist bazaar brochure.
Below: The author has abandoned his two-tone Austin Cambridge in the 'rump' of Ludgate Street in April 1968 to photograph the grandeur of Wellington Road. (NW)

'OLD-SOL' POLISH

SOLD IN TINS ONLY

OLD ✦ SOL
ANTISEPTIC & DAMP PROOF
FURNITURE, FLOOR & LINO
POLISH

IT DAZZLES!

FOR FURNITURE OF ANY DESCRIPTION, FLOORS & LINO.

IT IS EASY, QUICK & ECONOMICAL.

RAYBOULD, WHITEHOUSE & Co Ltd

MANUFACTURING CHEMISTS

Wellington Rd.

DUDLEY.

Telephone 2124 } 2 lines   Established
2237   1878.

Stafford Street curves through the right hand side of this postcard aerial view, on its way up to Top Church. On the left is Wolverhampton Street. Southalls Lane and Cross Street are also very visible but the top of Wellington Road is obscured by buildings. The picture shows how densely Dudley was built-up, although St. James's Road, on the extreme left has no houses on the right hand side! (Ken Rock Collection)

Southall's Lane also appears on the Treasure's map of 1835 - running from Wolverhampton Street across to the junction of Stafford Street and Wellington Road - seen here from the corner of Cross Street looking towards The King and Queen. (Anon contributor)

Right: The King & Queen was a handsome pub with a tiled exterior to the ground floor. It was photographed here in 1980 shortly before it closed and was converted into flats. Modern apartments have also replaced the row of cottages seen above, although the Wolverhampton Street end of Southall's Lane is relatively unchanged. (NW)

Stafford Street has lost most of its historical buildings but the Dudley Joinery, Sawing, Planing and Moulding Mill survives as the Dudley Snooker and Pool Club! This started life as the headquarters of Nelson's the builders and was then enlarged into this form when taken over by Messrs. Oakley and Coulson so that the latter could make their own joinery on the premises as well as store building materials. At one time it stood next door to Price's bakery and the Midland Counties Dairy but these landmarks have disappeared.

Behind the joinery works is another "sub-section" of Dudley bordered by Stafford Street, Wellington Road, Russell Street and Grange Road. In the centre of this area were once the Park Schools. Some Edwardian housing survives in streets like Edward Street and Alexandra Street, now separated from "The New Dock" by these tower blocks.

This terrace - once with its own corner shop at the end, forms the top of Maughan Street. The New Dock itself was divided into two parts. One section consisted of Himley Street, Lawley Street and Maughan Street. The other part consisted of Swan Street, Holland Street, Waterloo Street and St. Luke's Terrace, which began life as "Thirteen House Row". Into this area came the Congregationalists to build a mission, first in Maughan Street, and then, in this guise, in Himley Street by the corner of Grange Park. (NW)

The Congregationalists from Waddam's Pool established a "mission" in Lawley Street, in the New Dock, in the 1870s. It was led by Thomas Amos, seen here cutting the sod to commence the building of the new Park Congregational Church in April 1906.

This church was to replace the Lawley Street mission, and another in Maughan Street, and an independent group from Steppingstone Street. The church opened on 17th October 1906.

The extensive oak panelling which is such a striking feature of the interior even today, was not added until the 1930s. (The organ had been added in 1929.)

Thomas Amos died in 1908 and was followed by A.T. Price - seen above. He came from Salop Street Methodists and led the folks at Park until his death in 1933.

Left: Here we see the congregation celebrating their centenary in October 2006.

Chapter 7
What's Behind Top Church?

For a time during the late 1960s Dudley advertised itself as, "For Zoo, Shopping and Car Parks". The slogan used to appear on carefully franked mail despatched from Dudley and must have amused those who felt you could make a virtue of free car parking. Now that we have to pay for that commodity we realise it was indeed a virtue. At the time, anyone coming to explore these car parks would have been rewarded by finding acres of tarmac just behind the town's centre and a new footbridge waiting to transfer you to the Churchill Precinct and thus into the town centre.

Much of this parking space was created by the clearance of the Flood Street area - a lengthy process that began in the late 1920s and was completed by the mid 1960s. It involved the wholesale demolition of many streets of densely built nineteenth century housing and factories, and moving the residents to new council homes on estates such as The Priory. Flood Street was only one such street but it gave its name to the area, and by the time I was exploring the area all that remained was the Ghost of Flood Street - and the 'legend.'

The urbanisation of the Flood Street area was well underway as the nineteenth century expansion of

Dudley unfolded, and it can be seen clearly on Treasure's Map of 1835 as a triangular area bordered by King Street, Vicar Street and Oakeywell Street. The latter sides of the triangle converged at the point where Dudley built its gasworks alongside the 'green-sounding' Spring Gardens. But generally there was nothing "green" about the Flood Street area. It was low-lying, unsanitary, unplanned, and overcrowded. As further testimony to its early development, the Primitive Methodists had sent in their missionaries and established a chapel in George Street as early as 1829. Today you would have difficulty identifying its location. The street names have been obscured by new buildings as well as the car parks. Falcon House, for example, quotes its address as 'The Minories' and I have heard people use the place name, 'The Mamble', but I guess that no one hopes that these terms conjure up pictures of depressing slums! There are a few street name boards still welcoming explorers to places like Constitution Hill or Tetnall Street, but the arrival of the Dudley Southern Bypass has further complicated the attempt to picture the Flood Street area as it was.

One way of trying to picture the area as it was is to explore the surviving streets that once stood aloof

The most obvious answer to the question: "What's behind Top Church?" is: "The Vicarage." This attractive building was built in 1930 to replace an earlier Victorian vicarage on the corner of Vicar Street and King Street, just behind the church.
It was designed by Messrs. Webb & Grey - Dudley based architects who designed many local buildings.

Unfortunately, it is another example of a Dudley building that seems to have been allowed to deteriorate.

(2007 photograph: NW)

Above: Henry Oakes' shop at 47 Flood Street at the turn of the century. Henry stands in front of his shop with wife Eliza, daughters Mary Ann and Clara, and his nephew Joshua Banks. (Megan Crofts)

Below: Mrs. Winchurch in front of her shop at 58 Flood Street in 1963, surrounded by signs of "clearance" but determined to carry on selling everything. (Dudley Archives & local History Centre)

This building housed the works canteen of The Dunlop Rim & Wheel Company - the scene of my first visit to the Flood Street area while working for the Department of Employment in 1966. Seen here in 2007, it is now home to a Hindu Temple. This corner of Hope Street and Churchfield Street has been the scene of much industry hinted at by names like The Queens Cross Anvil & Vice Works, and The Churchfield File Mills. (NW)

from Flood Street, and were built on higher ground more directly behind Top Church. Abberley Street was just beginning to be developed when Treasure's map was drawn and today has the least nineteenth century atmosphere to be found in this enclave. However, if you continue your exploration into Brooke Street and Hellier Street you find late nineteenth century development that was still going on when the 1901 OS map was being drawn, now available to us all in the Alan Godfrey series. Some elegant villas jostle with more modest terraced housing and strange 'building lines' echo field boundaries of an earlier age. Again this little area is triangular - bordered by Churchfield Street, Hope Street and Vicar Street. Industrial premises also jostle for space in and around the housing in a way that must have once characterised Flood Street. I first encountered this when working for the Employment Exchange and we had to go to the works of the Dunlop Rim & Wheel Company to pay out short time working subsidy. We made our way into a works canteen, which is now a Hindu Temple!

Just as you would once have stumbled across the Prims in George Street, or a couple of other 'missions' established in the Flood Street area, nowadays it is possible to stumble across the Hellier Street Gospel Hall - one of Dudley's most "hidden" places of worship! Of course, it is not really hidden at all but on two occasions when I have taken people to visit the hall they have all encountered it with a sense of surprise. The key person involved in

building this little gospel hall was Evan Griffiths who ran a herbalist shop in King Street. He died in December 1930 and the hall bears the date "1931" suggesting he did not live to see his hall completed.

It is interesting that when it comes to looking at the territory behind Top Church, it is not the buildings that beg to be remembered - it is person. That person is Bert Bissell (1902 - 1998). What he built in the Flood Street area was "The Young Men's Bible Class", forever associated with the chapel in Vicar Street. The chapel itself had been a replacement for the old Primitive Methodist Chapel in George Street. It opened in 1902 near the corner of Vicar Street and Martin Hill Street. Work started just as the Second World War began on adding a new building right on the corner of Martin Hill Street and in turn this became the chapel and the 1902 building was demolished. Worship is to cease in this building on 31st August 2008, just as this book "goes to press", and the Bible Class will have to find a new home. Bert Bissell is commemorated elsewhere in Dudley - with a little piece of Ben Nevis erected on the corner of Coronation Gardens, opposite the Council House - but when the Vicar Street chapel closes it symbolically ends a chapter of the Flood Street area's history.

Above left: A beautiful little warehouse still standing at 39 Churchfield Street.

Above right: This narrow "track" off Hellier Street follows a field boundary shown on Treasure's map of 1835. The hills at Abberley form the skyline.

Left: The Hellier Street Gospel Hall appears to slowly sink below the level of Hellier Street. Evan Griffiths bought this patch which had once just been a rubbish tip. The row of houses behind the hall are those seen top right.

(All pictures taken 2007 NW)

Left: The author, Ned Williams, stands above the baptismal pool in the Hellier Street Gospel Hall to address members of the Black Country Society on the occasion of the Society's visit to the area in May 2006. Most members of the party confessed to never having explored this part of Dudley and never having visited a gospel hall!

(Graham Beckley)

Above: The sisters, Evelyn and Iris Watson, daughters of Florence Watson, stand outside the door of their mother's shop on the corner of Hellier Street and Churchfield Street about 1930. (The shop was numbered as 18 Churchfield Street.) The family moved to the Priory Estate in 1933. Although the area around Flood Street was "cleared" this area has survived and this building can still be seen today although no longer operating as a corner shop. (Mike Evans)

Below: The Vicar Street "campus" in 1992, with the 1940 building and gates to Martin Hill Street. Behind this is the Sunday School building of 1902, at the right hand end of which was "the Institute". It must have been demolished soon after this picture was taken. The 1902 building was nearer Church Street than either Vicar Street or Martin Hill Street, and the ground occupied by the 1940 building was for many years just open ground on which horses grazed! (Vicar Street Archives)

Bert Bissell

As far as I know, I never met Bert Bissell, but in the process of exploring Dudley I can almost be persuaded that did in fact meet him! His name, and his presence, has popped up everywhere and many Dudley folk have included a reference to Bert in the information they have passed on to me whatever their other interests in Dudley. Bert's biography was put together by his nephew, Don Bissell, in a 1997 publication: "God's Mountaineer", but I doubt whether the full story has yet been told.

Bert Bissell was born on 9th January 1902 in Goole, Yorkshire, one of the six sons of a Methodist minister, although the family stressed its Black Country ancestry - with a background in the industries of the Halesowen area, and in the service of Primitive Methodism. His father, Joseph Bissell (1869 - 1931) worked in many Black Country chapels as well as in other parts of Britain. After Joseph's death the Bissells moved to a council house in Selbourne Road - with which Bert was associated for the rest of his life and in which he lived alone after the death of his mother in 1952. The house was later called "Ben Nevis".

Bert's working life began in Coventry but the Black Country connection was strengthened when his father took on the ministry at Bent Street, Brierley Hill. It was there that Bert gained his first experience of running a "Young Men's Bible Class." His father then moved to Dudley and step by step Bert took on the mission of running a Young Men's Bible Class at Vicar Street. The class first met in mid September 1925 in the "Institute" - a fairly primitive extension to the Vicar Street chapel of 1902.

Eventually Bert relinquished his work in Coventry (house to house credit sales of footwear and drapery) and focussed all his attention on Vicar Street, where the class began to flourish. For a time he was 'lay pastor' of the chapel for £1.50 a week but his life took on another dimension when he was able to become Dudley's first (part-time) Probation Officer. Don Bissell's biography charts all the twists and turns in Bert's life including his encounter with Edward Jeffreys when the latter brought his evangelistic crusade to Dudley Town Hall in 1930.

From the late twenties onwards The Vicar Street Young Men's Bible Class becomes the main thread of Bert's story with his work for the Probation

Inderjit Bhogal and Bert Bissell outside the Vicar Street Chapel. Inderjit had joined the class in 1965, and this picture was taken ten years later when the group was celebrating its 50th Anniversary.

Service coming second. It became more widely know and appreciated after the events of 1945 when Bert and members of the class erected a Peace Cairn on the summit of Ben Nevis. Through Bert's work, links were established between Dudley and Coventry, and Fort William and far off Japan.

Bert himself believed in the value of creating a photographic archive and a great many pictures survive relating to the life and times of Vicar Street, the Bible Class with all its anniversaries, activities, and constant assaults on Ben Nevis and all the "peace work" in which he became engaged. The latter activities took Bert all over the world. Recognition of Bert's work and achievement ranged from an MBE to the Freedom of the Borough of Dudley, plus many other international awards.

Bert Bissell died in 1998 and is buried in Glen Nevis cemetery, in the shadow of the Ben. There were funeral services in both Fort William and Vicar Street, Dudley. The latter was led by Rev. Inderjit Bhogal who had once been a member of the Young Men's Bible Class, but by then was President of the Methodist Conference.

This picture of the Vicar Street Young Men's Bible Class was taken on 11th. April 1926 - only about eight months after Bert had started the group with only four potential members at the first meeting. The picture provides another tantalising glimpse of the 1902 building - erected by the Primitive Methodists after vacating their 1829 chapel down in George Street.
It is possible to locate Bert Bissell, seated with his arms folded, near the centre of the group.

Bert Bissell unveils a plaque to commemorate the laying of the foundation stone on 14th October 1939 for the "new" chapel at Vicar Street. The chapel provided the usual range of services on Sunday and a Sunday School, but Bert Bissell's Young Men's Bible Class seems to have dominated the life of the chapel as it met several nights during the week as well as on Sunday afternoon. Bert organised a bewildering range of activities for these meetings.

(Photos from the Vicar Street Archives)

Left: Dudley's first woman Mayor, Councillor Kate Rodgers brings a Japanese delegation into Vicar Street in February 1972 to meet Bert Bissell and accept two inscribed "peace tablets" to be taken to Hiroshima. (One tablet came from Vicar Street, the other from Fort William. this was to return a gesture from the Japanese when, in 1968, thay had sent a tablet to be incorporated into the cairn on Ben Nevis.) In 1978 Bert was able to make a 16 day visit to Japan in the cause of peace.

The last service was held at Vicar Street on Sunday 31st. August 2008. Below: Half an hour to go and most seats already taken!

Left: The last service was led by Rev. Jennifer Hurd, John Mundon, Rev. David Monkton, Dalton Bruce St. John, Alan Wedge, Astley Blake, and Rev. Inderjit Bhogal - seen here standing outside the chapel after the service. (All the chaps had once been members of Bert Bissell's Men's Bible Class) Missing from the picture is Dorothy Morgan who had led the opening prayers. (NW)

Chapter 8
Holly Hall, and Woodside

Holly Hall was originally a small settlement stretching along the Stourbridge Road near St. Augustine's Church. The road junction by this church was presumably the starting point of the turnpike road connecting Dudley with Worcester dating from the end of the eighteenth century. The hamlet of Woodside would seem to have developed with the coming of the Woodside Ironworks - built up in the 1840s on land leased by the Cochrane Family from the Earl of Dudley, and close to the turnpike road and the canal. The irony appears to be that the ironworks and the village were not quite on each other's doorstep so it is puzzling to try and account for the development of Woodside. The coming of the Pensnett Canal, running from Parkhead to the Wallows, and the arrival of the Oxford, Worcester and Wolverhampton Railway in 1852 add to the puzzle. A station was not provided at Woodside until 1895 and then claimed to serve both Woodside and Harts Hill. Possibly little used, the station was closed in 1916 as a wartime economy and never re-opened. (Currently, in 2008, the location of the station is the northern limit of the headshunt of the rail access still provided to the Round Oak Steel Terminal.)

The late nineteenth century Woodside was quite compact, and was well provided with Methodist chapels. The main roads were High Street (now Highgate Road), Hall Street (now Hallchurch Road) and Cross Street (Now Crossgate Street) running between them. Cross Street led to the Square and the layout of this street and the Square itself suggest late nineteenth century planning, contrasting with the less-planned settlement of the area between The Square and the railway. Wood Street and The Croft, on the 1900 map, look like unplanned developments of the mid-nineteenth century. The area changed again when inter-war house building began to join Woodside to Holly Hall; a process which was continued after the war. "Holly Hall Road" was built from the Clee Road area right into the heart of Woodside at The Square, and at first was home to post-war pre-fabs. So - how did a Londoner exiled to Eve Hill in the 1960s find himself exploring this area?

Sometime early in 1964 I ceased to be a resident of St. George's Hall at Dudley Training College and became a 'day student' which involved finding somewhere local to live. This was the result of a difference of opinion with the Principal, David Jordan, an episode best described by that phrase, "and that's another story."

51 Pensnett Road, Holly Hall. The flat in the cellar and rear of this building was the author's home from 1964 until 1974. It was rented from The Low Town Launderette Co. represented by Mrs. Hilda Gardner who ran the shop-next-door - seen on the left of the picture. The 1901 map, reproduced in the Alan Godfrey series, shows this building and the mirror-image building to the right of 51 as almost the westernmost limits of the original Low Town. As such they were the only surviving buildings of Low Town from the 1960s onwards until their demolition in the Autumn of 2006. Mrs. Gardner's shop and the building next door were 1950s replacements for the former Low Town buildings on that site, and the main thoroughfare of Low Town was just beyond them. (NW)

Top left: The rear view of 51 and 53 Pensnett Road about 1965. Lowtowners talk of 51 as the home of Victor Smith, and 53 of the Farley family. The latter still occupied 53 while I lived at 51. We were just "incomers" and do not seem to count in the history of Low Town, because by then the main portion of Low Town had been demolished and the residents dispersed.
Bottom left: Life in the car port at the back of 51 in 1965. Bernard Barnes paints and my 350cc Triumph motor cycle rests between journeys of Black Country exploration. (NW)

It was not easy to find flats in the Dudley of the mid 1960s, especially if funds were limited. I saw some terrible premises in Himley Road and Wellington Road before joining forces with fellow-student Bernard Barnes in placing an advertisement in the Express & Star. We described ourselves as 'teachers' rather than 'students' and stressed the need for somewhere quiet, hoping to sound very respectable. This must have worked because we were phoned by Bert Cooksey and asked to come an inspect rooms at 51 Pensnett Road, Holly Hall.

51 Pensnett Road was a Victorian house on the edge of Low Town. The main portion of the house had been converted into four bed-sitters, but we were offered 'the flat'. Because the premises were built on sloping ground this flat consisted of a cellar, an adjoining yard which had been covered with a corrugated carbonate roof, and the former outbuildings which had become toilet, bathroom and small bedroom which also contained the 'kitchen sink'. The sink was at the opposite end of the complex to the gas stove in the cellar! It was designed for communal living and could only be occupied by those who cared little for privacy, or comfort and warmth.

We happily accepted it and found that we had become tenants of the Low Town Launderette Company - a business established by Bert Cooksey, a builder, and Mrs. Gardner who owned the shop next door. At first the rent was £3 a week shared between two of us.

Moving to the Low Town part of Holly Hall opened up many new ways of appreciating Dudley, and at last we were citizens of Dudley rather than aliens living in a student ghetto up on Eve Hill. There was much to learn.

The inmates of the bedsitters upstairs told us how we could obtain coal to fill our grate. We had to set off armed with buckets and had to head down the track through what had once been Low Town towards Fens Pool. On reaching the Earl of Dudley's railway line we had to turn left and "walk

Right: An electric tramcar on the Dudley-Stourbridge service passes Saint Augustine's Church, Holly Hall about 1910.

Note the drinking fountain donated to the local community to commemorate the wife of Brooke Robinson who died in 1892. (Netherton and Woodside had to be treated alike so a similar fountain was provided in Netherton.) The fountain was removed in 1954.

St. Augustine's church was completed in 1884, and forms a focal point to Holly Hall, linking the community along the main road with the older settlement of Woodside.

(From a postcard in the collection of John Smith)

Right: The interior of St. Augustine's Church has a dark medieval quality, unlike the lightness of St. James' and St. John's. (Val Davies Collection)

Below: A St. Augustine's "Nativity" of 1948 or 1949, photographed by the Vicar, Rev. Erasmus Aubrey Davenport Naylor, who had an entrepreneurial side line in taking photos of such events and selling prints to parishioners.
(Margaret Pearce Collection)

the sleepers" to the sidings near The Wallows. In these sidings were rows of coal wagons and loco-motive tenders that were awaiting scrapping. Here was a ready supply of coal! Scrapping the wagons proceeded quickly and therefore the supply ceased and we had to heat the cellar from then on with a paraffin heater.

Meanwhile this episode had introduced me to the Earl's railway, but foolishly I took it all for granted. I have vague memories of one of Jack Aldiss's tours of Dudley in the Autumn of 1962 bringing us up the main road past The Wallows, and seeing steam loco-motives 'on shed', but by 1964 the line was dieselised and only one train per day seemed to crawl from The Wallows across our line to the Old Park Engineering Works. I never photographed this train, but the wooden wagons bearing the letters "ED" (Earl of Dudley) and PR (Pensnett Railway) lasted long enough to feature in one of our cine films.

Setting out from 51 Pensnett Road to explore the features of the local environment took me in two directions. Setting out towards Pensnett led to the fascinating world of Barrow Hill and St. Mark's churchyard. The evening walk to Barrow Hill enabled us to witness many stunning sunsets, and on the far side of St. Mark's churchyard was another 'wonder' of the Earl of Dudley's railway system: The Barrow Hill Incline.

Setting out in the other direction, crossing the main road by St. Augustine's Church, led through Woodside, over the railway line, and into Blackbrook Road. Later the section of this road between the railway bridge and Peartree Lane was cut off and incorporated into Gadd's premises, and later still the access from Peartree Lane became more obscured. This has been a pity because traversing Blackbrook Road was an interesting adventure!

For the motor-cyclist there was something exciting about setting out for Netherton by this back route as the canal bridge half way along the lane was spectacularly hump-backed. I once lost control of the bike on this bridge - my only experience of being on a motorbike travelling backwards down a steep slope. Close to this bridge there had once been a pub called The Barley Mow in the middle of nowhere, but marking the border between Netherton and Woodside.

My reason for travelling to Netherton was to take part in the activities of the Cine Section of Dudley Photographic Society. The Cine Section met in a

film studio created in the attic of Little's Shoe Factory. It was there that I met a fellow film-maker of my own age named Michael Ball, and, as Uralia Films took shape in its "offices" at 51 Pensnett Road, he became the resident sound engineer.

Amateur film-making gained momentum at the same time as I found myself exploring Barrow Hill, Woodside and Netherton, but our concern was to tell stories, not to use our cameras to record the changing local environment. Parkhead also soon became one of our favourite locations: it had everything one could wish for: canals and a canal tunnel, a railway viaduct, and towpaths that led to many other wonderful locations.

Right on our own doorstep was Low Town itself. There was very little to see by the mid 1960s apart from a few crumbling brick walls buried in long grass, and the main thoroughfare was becoming very overgrown - despite the fact that the entrance is still marked by a road-sign today - forty years later. Once the entrance to Low Town was flanked by the King William IV, but a new pub of the same name had been built on the other side of the Pensnett Road in the 1920s. In Low Town itself there had once been The Jolly Collier. We were told that it had existed until 1960 but that seemed unlikely. We were also told stories of ghosts and exorcisms at The Jolly Collier! I took this up in my very first article for The Blackcountryman some years later.

Below: Holly Hall's "city centre" captured in an Edwardian postcard view. To the left: Hall Street (now Hallchurch road) and to the right: High Street (now Highgate Road - a main approach road to Merry Hill!). The Victorian school building was provided by Mr. A.B.

Cochrane and opened on 3rd June 1861 and was later bought from his estate by the Earl of Dudley and absorbed into the Dudley School Board's jurisdiction. This building was demolished in 1987. The shop on the right was Holly Hall's first post office. (John Smith Clln.)

The Holly Hall Branch of the Dudley Co-operative Society in Stourbridge Road, probably photographed in the 1920s. It was here that Manager Jack Edge welcomed me to the Co-operative Society in 1965. When the Birmingham Co-operative Society took over the Dudley Society in 1982, small branches such as this were closed. (Co-op Collection)

H. Rumsey Williams' pharmacy was photographed in October 1985. It was on the corner of Stourbridge Road and Holly Street. Holly Street, Kinver Terrace and the Holly Hall Secondary School were the only developments on this side of the Stourbridge Road until after the First World War. (NW)

Although we made enquiries about Low Town, and occasionally drank in The King William IV, we met very few people who could tell us much about our local 'vanished village'. Its 'clearance' at the end of the 1940s, and subsequent demolition, seemed to have resulted in the dispersal of those who had lived there, and perhaps people had not yet learned to value talking about the past - "local history" was still to be properly invented. As it turned out the Low Towners had not gone far and were probably still to be found in Holly Hall or on the Russells Hall Estate. It is therefore very pleasing that in recent times they have emerged and have been brought back together to put the story of Low Town "on the record". Val Worwood and Michael Smith led others in producing a book about Low Town, and Arthur Edwards has built an excellent model of the township (see page 96.)

At the top of Pensnett Road was a little triangle of buildings forming a junction with the Stourbridge Road, and included a little garage run by the Phillips family. It was all swept away soon after I had moved to 51 Pensnett Road and this may have led to the first stirrings of that feeling: "I should have recorded that". The gradual awareness that there was such a thing as local history at first led people to go back into a distant past, only later did it become apparent that recording the present was going to be vital to the next generation of local historians. Questioning people, collecting memories, exploring everywhere, and recording everything demanded a confidence that I lacked in 1964 despite being nosy and enjoying such exploration. The formation of the Black Country Society in 1967 changed everything - suddenly a group of people existed who responded to 'change' by encouraging an active interest in everything 'local'.

The Woodside Library in Stourbridge Road, Holly Hall in 2008. Provision of this library and the adjoining fire station and police houses ran parallel to the provision of similar facilities in Netherton. Both libraries opened on 24th July 1894.

The Woodside building is slightly more modest but is obviously the work of the same architect, Tom Grazebrook, and builder, Messrs. Willets of Old Hill. (In both cases land was provided by the Earl of Dudley specifically for this purpose.) The library was closed on 6th September 2008. (NW)

The Holly Hall Fish & Chip Shop in the Stourbridge Road, photographed in the 1980s, occupied premises in a very solid row of late Victorian houses that stretched towards Harts Hill from below the Library. The shop was run by various families including the Phillips who had moved here when the little "triangle" of buildings at the top of Pensnett Road was demolished about 1964. Later the Harris family served the fish and chips. Today (2008) it is a Chinese 'Take-away'.
(Sue Hazleton)

The last surviving building of Holly Hall Secondary School, Stourbridge Road, looks very forlorn in 2008. It was once the cookery department. The school, originally opened as Harts Hill Baord School in 1875, was replaced by a brand new Holly Hall Secondary School at Scotts Green which opened on 26th September 1966.
(Sue Hazleton)

Above: From the top of Hall Street, now Hallchurch Road, one looks down through Woodside and across the Black Brook valley towards Netherton. (Saint. Andrew's Church is silhoueted on the horizon). To the left is the roof of Woodside Wesleyan Methodist Chapel. In the centre is the roof of the chapel in The Square. (Sue Hazelton)

Left: The Crown Inn at the junction of High Street and Wood Street, January 1971. It has since been replaced by a modern building facing Highgate Road. (NW)

Left: The Railway Tavern still occupies its nineteenth century premises in what is now called Buxton Road, but which was originally part of "The Croft". (NW)

Woodside Wesleyan Methodists first built a chapel in Hall Street as early as 1812, but the building seen here was built in the1890s. As the Methodist congregations at The Square, Mount Zion and Harts Hill "closed" they have all been absorbed into the surviving congregation in what is now called Hallchurch Road.

Right: On 11th May 2008 the Sunday School children assemble outside the chapel before going in to celebrate the Sunday School Anniversary in modern style.

Below: Like many local chapels, Woodside contains bricks bought by local supporters at the time of building the premises, their names preserved for posterity. (NW)

Right: The Sunday School Anniversary in fullswing at the Woodside Methodist Chapel on 9th May 2004. Even this is now a historical picture as the wooden pews seen in this picture have now been replaced with modern chairs, and the interior of the chapel has been refurbished. This followed a short period when it looked as if some subsidence might cause the chapel to close. (NW)

Right: Both St. Augustine's Church and the Methodist chapels liked to parade around Woodside on Sunday School anniversaries. With the chapel in The Square on the left, their Sunday School sets out along Holly Hall Road in the 1960s. (Roy Evans)

The Primitive Methodists built their first chapel in Woodside in The Croft, backing on to the railway, after 'missionary work' by the Prims in George Street in the 1830s.

Later they moved to The Square, and opened this chapel in 1882. The foundation stones were laid on 3rd April by Job Garratt (Mayor of Dudley) and two others. Twelve years later on 12th November 1894, three more stones were laid as work began on the Sunday School behind this building. The Woodside Brass Band, led by Mr. Addis, attended on both occasions. (NW)

This picture taken in the 1960s shows the Boys Brigade lining up outside the chapel for an Anniversary parade. The company, later the 1st Dudley Company, was formed in 1952 as the 10th South Staffs Co. The picture also provides a glimpse of the old shops 'next door' - now replaced with a small modern parade.
(Roy Evans)

Inside the Methodist chapel on The Square, Woodside, at a 1960s anniversary, facing the platform and the organ. When this chapel closed most of the remaining congregation transferred to Hallchurch Road.

In 1980 the building, in fairly derelict condition, was bought by the New Testament Church of God and reopened on 23rd May 1981. The organ seen here was later removed and recently the chapel has been modernised. (Roy Evans)

Rev. Osborne Johns admires the foundation stone laid by Mayor Job Garratt, now preserved in the new entrance to the chapel in The Square - now home to the New Testament Church of God. This chapel was re-dedicated on Saturday 30th August 2008. The NTCofG started in the UK in Wolverhampton in 1953, and was brought to Dudley by Rev. Gilbert Peddie in 1958. After occupying a number of homes, the congregation came to Woodside in 1981. (NW)

THIS STONE WAS LAID
BY
JOB GARRATT ESQ
MAYOR OF DUDLEY
APRIL 3rd 1882

Below left: The Congregational Chapel in High Street, Woodside was built in 1844 and lasted until 1974. This picture was taken just before closure. It backed onto the pit banks that were turned into the park. (K. Mole)
Below right: Mount Zion - the home of the New Connexion Methodists in Woodside with an entrance facing High Street. (Mabel Blewitt)

Job Garratt

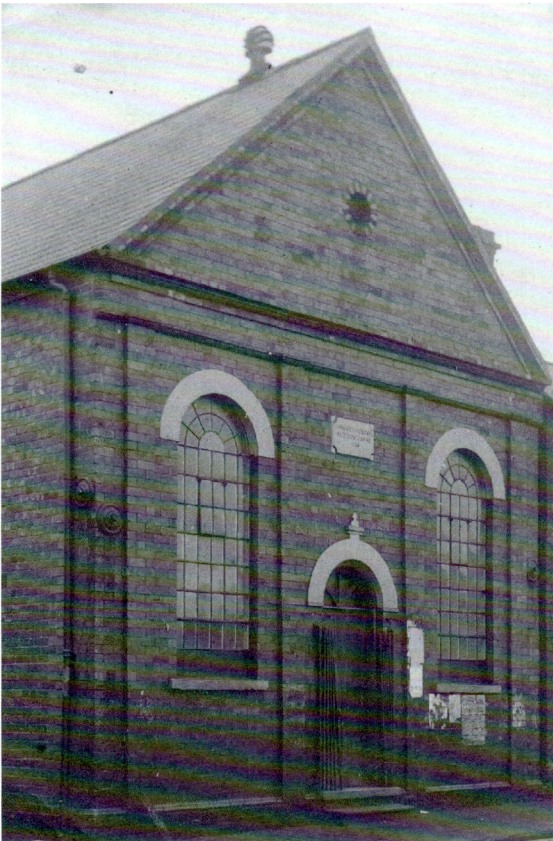

Left: Thomas Jone's Fair in Woodside Park on 10th August 2008 - from 'the bank' looking towards Avenue Road. (NW)
Below left: Peter Marson plays bowls in Woodside Park c. 1960. (Marjorie Clarke)
Below right: The huge memorial fountain in memory of Job Garratt still tucked away in Woodside Park in 2008. (NW)

Left - top of opposite page: Woodside Park, 1960. Once again the photographer stands on the bank looking down into the lower part of the park - compare with the view of the fair which is standing on ground to the right of this area. Avenue Road is just beyond the playground, and Netherton church is on the skyline. The Job Garratt memorial is just to the left, partly obscured by trees.
The park was developed around 1902 - firstly as a recreation ground reclaimed from pit banks. (Parallel to the development of Netherton Park.) Bill Bawden

Top of this page: The Croft; a track that began here by "The Station Bridge" and swung round towards The Square. Some of the oldest houses in Woodside were to be found in The Croft, suggesting this is where the settlement began. The picture was taken on 25th April 1951 just before this railway line was about to celebrate its centenary. The Stourbridge Jct. - Dudley line closed to passengers in 1962 and completely in 1993. (Michael Hale)

The memorial (opposite page) to Job Garratt (1839 - 1908) was unveiled on 28th. October 1911 by the Mayor, Alderman J.A.Hillman.

Right: Peter Marson poses by his Austin A35, and with his nephew, outside Kinver Terrace in 1969. We are looking along the terrace towards the Stourbridge Road. These houses were compulsorily purchased and demolished in the mid 1970s. Behind the terrace was a six-foot drop, overlooking the houses in The Hollies, some of which were "back to back". Peter Marson recalls his life in Holly Hall on the next page.

Growing up in Holly Hall

Peter Marson was born in September 1940 and grew up in the family home in Kinver Terrace - an unadopted street of twelve houses at right angles to the main Stourbridge Road, almost opposite the library. (See page 85). He recalls:

"One of my earliest memories was watching a Spitfire or a Hurricane up in the sky chasing a German bomber that had come to bomb "The Earl's", in about 1943. Despite the distance from "The Earl's", we could hear the bull in Holly Hall announcing the beginning and end of shifts - at 6.00.am, 2.00.pm and 10pm.: we could set our clocks by it.

I started school at Holly Hall Infants where Miss Chambers was in charge and went on to the Juniors where Mr. Duffle was the Head, known to everyone as "Daddy Duffel". I passed the 11+ and went off to Dudley Grammar School - to be followed three years later by Mr. Duffel! What I remember about the 11+ exam was that it was interrupted by a teacher coming in to tell us that King George VI had died. I also remember the Herald - in full costume - coming to make a proclamation of the Queen's accession from the steps of Holly Hall Library.

As a child growing up in Holly Hall I found no shortage of places to go. The park was immaculate, looked after by three gardeners and a park keeper. The facilities included tennis courts and a bowling green, as well as cricket and football pitches. Our main stamping ground was the Old Park, reached by making our way down Pensnett Road, past Low Town where we were told the Chopper Gang was inhabiting The Jolly Collier, and into the Old Park by the railway bridge. I don't ever remember seeing a train on that stretch of the Earl's railway, but we did see trains on the stretch that led up the bridge and watched them tip slag from the wagons.

The Old Park was a vast wilderness, some of which was wooded, some of which was still covered with the remains of old pits. We could set off with our snap (sandwiches made by Mum) and spend the whole day there. We also sometimes helped gather the harvest at Hollies Farm on the land now occupied by Russell's Hall Hospital.

We also used to go down to "The Broads" - the name we gave to a sleeper-built fence that separated the railway from The Croft. We sat on this fence and enjoyed some train-spotting. Occasionally we walked to the workshops at The Wallows on the Earl's railway system, and nobody seemed to mind us wandering around to have a look! Another journey in that direction was to the saw mill operated by Robert Matthews & Son at Harts Hill. On one side of the Stourbridge Road were huge piles of logs, on the other the huge saws were at work.

I also remember the Sunday School parades led by the Vicar at St. Augustine's church - sometimes going down as far as Harts Hill where there was a Mission Church. The parade would stop now and again and the Vicar would preach, sometimes from a chair, and sometimes from somebody's bedroom window! The Vicar, the Rev. E.A.D. Naylor, once commented on the strange Christian names some parents chose for their children, which seemed rich coming from someone called Erasmus Aubrey Devonport!

Once in our teens we could go off to the cinemas in Dudley or Brierley Hill, but most of the time our social lives could be filled by the amount of activity going on at the church and local chapels. At St. Augustine's we had a Young Mens' Club led by Dave Kitchen which met in the church hall - an old First World War wooden building which was vast enough to accommodate a snooker table and table-tennis table at one end. Holly Hall teams played in a number of local leagues.

Mabel and George Bishop pose on the front step of their new home at 15 Surrey Road, on the Holly Hall Estate in 1950. It was "heaven with all mod-con". They had moved here from Kinver Terrace, having watched the house being built on land they had formerly called "The Fold". (Mabel Blewitt)

Old Woodside

Holly Hall and Woodside have changed so much, and the only way I can try to create a picture of the village as it was is to listen to those who knew it in the past and can still recall it in some detail. One person who still lives in the area today (2008) is Miss Doris Clarke who was born in a house in High Street in 1922. The back of her house overlooked the park, but between the house and the park was the Holly Hall ropewalk, operated by Ben Whitehouse well into the 1930s.

Doris can recall all the houses and shops of old Woodside and supplied this information. "At the Stourbridge Road end of High Street stood the Post Office run by Miss Millington. (See page 83) Descending High Street on the park side we came to Miss Capewell's and then Mrs. Danks. Both shops, like most of the others in the area, sold sweets and a few other items. Next to Miss Danks' was the congregational Chapel, followed by the entrance to the park. Houses then extended from there down to the Avenue Road junction, interupted at some point by a shop that sold the rope from the ropiary already mentioned. Beyond Avenue Road was Mr. Pearson, an undertaker, then premises that included Ellen Round's little drapery and Jack Wood's barbers shop and newsagency. Just before Cochrane Road there was Jim Dainty's grocery shop.

Coming back up High Street on the other side were more little shops including Mr. Gallear's general stores, Perry's the butcher, Hilda Williams' grocery and then Phillips' on the corner of Cross Street. (Mr. Phillips owned the only car in Woodside!) They sold "everyhting" and were related to the Phillips who had premises in the "triangle" at the top of Pensnett Road. Above Cross Street the shops included Mrs. Rhodes' fish and chip shop, another shop run by Mr. Harry Gallear and another of those little 'general stores' run by Mrs. Box."

Miss Clarke could also name all the shops in Cross Street, Stourbridge Road and The Square, and Woodside's many pubs. Opposite her High Street home was a football pitch used by Woodside Football Team which was based at The Crown. Housing began to fill the open spaces in the 1930s, and Miss Clarke herself moved to a brand new private house in Newland Grove in 1938. The first council houses came to Woodside in Bradford Ave., Malvern Ave., and Fullwood Ave. After the war much more of old Woodside disappeared under new housing, both council provided and private.

Below: The Holly Hall ropewalk, hidden behind the houses that once stood in High Street, Woodside (now Highgate Road). (Sheila Aston)

Above: The Woodside Band about 1937, just after it had changed its name to the North Worcestershire Military Band. The band's conductor (centre of picture) was Howard Addis, who ran a grocery shop at 416 Stourbridge Road. he had joined the band in 1906 when he was ten! The front row includes Enoch Burton, Frank Loverock, Frank Tombs and Bill Burton.
(Margaret Pearce)

Centre: The Woodside Liberals about 1930. On the right: Jack Charington, 2nd from right: Howard Addis, 4th from right: Frank Round. Possibly on the bowling green behind the club.
(Margaret Pearce)

Left: Another Sunday School parade from the chapel in The Square sets off in the 1960s amidst the residential suburban landscape of Holly Hall built since the Second World War. (Roy Evans)

Above: the view from the air clearly illustrates the relationship between Woodside and Netherton and the journey described on page 83. In the foreground are the houses of Holly Hall Road, Buxton Road etc., and to the right one can see Highgate Road crossing the "Station Bridge" and swing left of Gadd's steelyards to pass the site of the Woodside Ironworks on its right. The Black Brook valley creates quite a green wedge beyond Peartree Lane and it is possible to pick out St. Andrew's Church, Lodge Farm and the Reservoir in the distance. On the extreme left is the Glazebrook Estate, Cinder Bank and the centre of Netherton. (Kieth Hodgkin's Collection)

Most of Holly Hall and Woodside reverberated to the sound of the hammers at The Dudley Drop Forging Company. The company came to Vine Street in 1923 and grew to become one of the largest independent drop forgers in the UK. It later became known as Dudley Die Forging and in 2000 became part of the Stoke Forging Group, and still fills the gap between Holly Hall and Harts Hill today.

Above and left are two "snaps" of the large hammers at "Dudley Drop". (Les Bywater)

Notes on The Cochranes and the Woodside Ironworks:

Alexander Brodie Cochrane was the son of a Thomas Cochrane who had come down to the West Midlands from Scotland, firstly to Ironbridge and then to Dudley, where he died in 1853. A.B.Cochrane worked for M.& W. Grazebrook as a furnace manager at their Netherton Ironworks (Pear tree Lane). His son had the same names so matters become confusing. A.B. Cochrane Junior, born in 1813, followed in his father's footsteps, but in 1840 was able to lease land, and possibly an existing "works" at Woodside from the Earl of Dudley. He was supported financially by Joseph Bramah, another engineer, and proceeded to build a foundry and furnaces at Woodside. A.B. Cochrane Jnr, and his wife Esther (Hughes) had thirteen children, ten of whom were boys, eight of which survived. The eight sons inherited the Woodside Ironworks when their father died in 1863.

From 1875 onwards the only sons actively engaged in running the ironworks were Charles and Joseph Bramah, joined by the latter's son Walter in 1896. The latter eventually managed the works, probably until it closed. Charles Cochrane was a respected authority on blast furnaces and was President of the Institute of Mechanical Engineers in 1889. He died in 1898. Joseph Bramah Cochrane married Alice Evers Swindell, with whom he lived at Pedmore Hall. He died in 1908.

The Woodside Ironworks produced architectural and structural ironwork, pipes and the famous post boxes, and became a major employer in the area. A. B. Cochrane seems to have favoured a disciplined workforce, but also was keen to be the public benefactor. The workforce was sometimes treated to excursions to see the fruits of their labour, and A.B. Cochrane Jnr. provided the school for his employee's children at Holly Hall in 1861. The Earl of Dudley bought this school from the eight sons of A.B. Cochrane in 1876.

Collieries associated with the Woodside Ironworks were known as the Woodside Collieries and covered an area extending from the Blackbrook Road Bridge right back to a pit close to the Stourbridge Road. The latter effectively separated Woodside from Harts Hill. The pits were connected by a 2ft. 8 1/2in. in gauge tramroad system, on which steam locomotives were introduced in the 1900s. Three Hunslet engines were named 'Woodside', 'Brodie' and 'Bramah', and there was a Peckett called Nelson. All were 0-4-0STs and they were scrapped in 1924 when some of the assets of the ironworks were auctioned. A picture of 'Brodie' and 'Bramah' can be found in Ray Shill's "Industrial Locomotives of the West Midlands (IRS 1992).

The works closed in 1921 and about 1924 they were bought by John Cashmore Ltd., of Great Bridge. It seems that for most of the inter-war period the works lay partly derelict, partly salvaged and some parts may have continued to be used. Southerns Ltd., the timber merchants, bought part of the site in 1939, and more recently C. Brown & Sons (steel stockholders) have used part of the site.

(Much of this information was drawn from an article in the Blackcountryman of Spring 1984 - written by A.T.C. Lavender and E.M. Lavender, who together researched local history in the Holly Hall area.)

Low Town

No portrait of the Holly Hall and Woodside area of Dudley would be complete without reference to Low Town.

Low Town was a distinct community in its own right quite separate from any other existing settlement. Its origins are obscure but it is shown quite clearly on the 1880s Ordnance Survey maps and the Alan Godfrey reprint of the 1901 map. (Dudley West). It was laid out within such a tight and well-defined boundary that it suggests the houses must have been built in a short period after a single land purchase, probably from the Earl of Dudley. This must have been sometime during the first half of the nineteenth century assuming that the line of Pensnett Road was defined by an Enclosure Act. The Pensnett Road is both a boundary of Low Town and a means of access to it, as Low Town's only thoroughfare was the track at right angles to Pensnett Road. The King William IV pub was adjacent to the junction, but the present-day pub, on the opposite side of the road, replaced it in 1915. The original King William was in existence in 1915 as a beerhouse, perhaps providing further proof of Low Town's early development. The Jolly Collier,

Above: The work of putting Low Town "back on the map" has been the work of the Lowtowners themselves. Val Worwood and Michael Smith and a host of others have worked together to produce a book called "Low Town, Holly Hall: The Last Generation" which brings together memories and family photographs from the village. On 11th March 2007 they "re-united" for a visit to the site of Low Town and they are seen here on the track that descended from Pensnett Road down into the cluster of sixty houses forming the Low Town communtiy. (NW)

Opposite page: Arthur Edwards has built a model of Low Town based on his vivid memories of the place and the available maps. This has been a vital tool in the business of explaining Low Town to those who never knew it. The author's own home (1964-74) appears in the top left hand corner of the model. (NW)

pub usually associated with Low Town, may have come later, as it does not seem to be listed until 1860.

The occupants of Low Town were mainly miners working in the pits of the "Old Park", and suffered the economic misery of the ups and downs of that industry. Later there was greater diversity but it remained a poor community living in poor quality housing. The Clearance Order was issued in 1947, and Low Town was gradually swept away.

In January 1982 Maud Revill takes the author to see her father's cinema at Harts Hill. Entering the site from Vine Street the patron would have passed the paybox and 'gas engine building' before coming to the cinema itself.

Maud and the author are standing in front of the door to the rewind room - separated, as legally required, from the projection room, the door to which is seen on the left. Although the auditorium was full of junk, the cinema was virtually complete, and lain out of use for over forty years. (Tom Hetherington)

Kate Williams waits for the next show outside the Harts Hill Limelight Cinema - as rebuilt brick by brick at the Black Country Living Museum. In its short life as a working cinema the Limelight used to advertise its programmes with large pictorial posters mounted on a hoarding at the end of Vine Street facing the Stourbridge Road. some of the cinema's posters survive. (NW)

Once upon a time motorway journeys were enlivened by the sight of a William Round truck advertising Dudley, and looking good in its bright red and vermillion livery.

William Round started the business in 1884 in "horse and cart" days, first in Cross Street and then at 34 Greystone Passage in The Dock. The move came to Harts Hill in the 1930s. In the process of expanding their premises the firm took over the site of the Limelight Cinema in January 1982. (NW)

Chapter 9
Harts Hill

Having arrived in Pensnett Road in 1964, and having tried to grapple with problems in defining where Holly Hall began and ended, and similarly where Woodside began and ended, I was dismayed to find that as Holly Hall petered out, somewhere near the point where Cochrane Road met the Stourbridge Road, there was yet another separate village waiting to be explored. This was Harts Hill.

Harts Hill is another little settlement where the Church of England was rivalled by chapels. A mission church existed on the main Stourbridge Road, which was a satellite of St. Augustine's. Ironically it had originally been a Methodist chapel. Meanwhile the Prims and Wesleyans were uncomfortably close to one another: one in Garrett Street (once known as Wood Street), and the other in Chapel Street. The brick Sunday School building of the former still exists and is in industrial use, but the chapels themselves, and the Mission, have disappeared.

Harts Hill consisted of Vine Street and Chapel Street (later Charter St.), running at right angles to the Stourbridge Road, and Garrett Street and Brick Kiln Street running parallel to the main road. The southernmost boundary of Harts Hill was a few yards south of Canal Street which gave access to the Harts Hill Iron Works before crossing Lord Ward's Canal to reach the Brierley Hill Iron Works, later trading as Messrs. Hill & Smith. Harts Hill was an industrial village, mainly of small over-crowded houses, dominated by the local works. There was some development on the other side of the Stourbridge Road, including Terrace Street and the Mission Church, but this never really felt like Harts Hill - an impression reinforced by the fact that it was in Staffordshire, and the Urban District of Brierley Hill - therefore nothing to do with Dudley, Worcestershire!

Most of the housing in Harts Hill had been cleared in the 1950s, but the village retained an interesting "secret". One of my most interesting Black Country adventures was the "discovery" of the Harts Hill Limelight Cinema in January 1982. At the time I was completing a book about Black Country cine-mas, but I knew that one part of the story was missing. From the licensing records in Dudley's archives, I knew that there had been a Harts Hill Limelight Cinema throughout he 1920s, at the rather strange address: 49a Vine Street. Visits to Vine Street had revealed nothing and although conversations in pubs confirmed the cinema's existence, the fate of the cinema and its story eluded me.

Some publicity in the Dudley Herald resulted in Maude Revill contacting me and she gave me an invitation to come and see her family's cinema. Given that I thought the building had long been demolished, Maude had a great surprise in store for me. We walked from her home in Cochrane Road round into Vine Street. We approached some gates I had previously ignored and made our way through an inconspicuous door in a wall, and there - in front of us - was The Limelight. Maude was exchanging contracts with William Round for the sale of the building the very next day, all of which added to the excitement of seeing the little hut-like cinema. We explored the cinema and Maude recalled as much of its history as possible.

The building was remarkably complete although many people would have objected that it looked very unlike a cinema. It certainly wasn't an Odeon but it still fulfilled all the legal obligations of being a licensed cinema. Its double doors had the required push-bolts etc, the rewind room was correctly separated from the projection room. The screen was still painted on the end wall. Outside were the pay-box and the gas-engine house and Maude's father's office. It made me feel as if I was Carter walking into Tutenkamun's tomb - so much still existed. The projection equipment, account books, one remaining tip-up seat, some benches, a gramophone once played by Maude and many other items were still to be seen. Some posters were still in the office, and some of John Revill's printing equipment, but unfortunately there was no film.

When Maude and her husband married during the Second World War they had asked her father, John Revill, to show a film and that was probably the last time a film was shown. By then it had already been closed for over a decade as it had never "converted" to sound. Maude's brother had filled it with aquariums and other household items during the 1940s and everything else remained mothballed. That evening I wrote to Ian Walden, Director of the Black Country Museum expressing the hope that the Limelight might be saved. Eventually it was.

Today Harts Hill is a densely industrialised area with little to suggest the existence of houses, pubs, shops, chapels and a cinema. The bus garage was just outside the village - on the Brierley Hill side of Canal Street, although the Manager's Office, dating back to tramway days, was in Harts Hill proper. The whole site had once been a tramway depot dating back to the 1890s. Midland Red adapted it to bus garage specification as their buses replaced the trams in 1925. It was rebuilt in 1931 and much modernised in 1964. It survives but is now in industrial use.

Growing Up in Harts Hill

Alan George was born in Brick Kiln Street, Harts Hill, in 1926. He lived with his parents and two brothers in a purpose-built shop about half-way along the street, surrounded by small 'one-room-down and one-room-up' type houses, some of which were arranged in yards. There were no houses on the opposite side of the road as the land between the road and Lord Ward's Canal was occupied by the Harts Hill Iron Works. Alan had no sense at the time that these were slums, but he was aware that Harts Hill was something of an isolated "island" - not quite joined to anything else in the outside world.

There were probably over forty houses in Brick Kiln Street, plus four pubs, but the family ran the only shop. Mrs. George ran the shop itself having probably gained an interest in shop-keeping from her mother who ran a little shop at the far end of Brierley Hill. While Sam George was in the Army during the First World War, she had converted the front room of her mother's house in Garratt Street into a tiny shop. When Sam George returned to Harts Hill he, at first, had no job. He used to help a confectioner called Mr. Silcox and went with him to Kidderminster Market. While there one day he bought a horse and cart - thanks to a loan from Mr. Silcox. A piece of land was then rented where a stable could be built and grazing could be provided for the horse. The piece of land was at the back of the tram depot and stretched from Canal Street to the canal. It was an old 'pit-bonk' created by a pit in the Saltwells Colliery series developed for the Earl of Dudley in the nineteenth century.

The horse and cart enabled Sam George to build up a green-grocery round, while Mrs. George built up business in the Brick Kiln Street premises. The Canal Street "bonk" developed into quite a smallholding where some vegetables could be grown and fowl could be kept. Alan had to contribute to the work of the family enterprise and one of his memories is of loading a hundredweight sack of potatoes onto a home-made barrow which he then hauled down to Hill & Smiths' works and across to their canteen. No time for enjoying the panoramic views from the top of the bonk across the railway lines and the Round Oak Steel Works. But there was time for boyhood adventures that took him along the towpath from the Canal Street bridge to the derelict part

Left: Sam George took his own photograph of the shop at 24/25 Brick Kiln Street, Harts Hill.
(Alan George collection)

Amongst the houses, small shops, and industry of Harts Hill were two chapels. Surprisingly the brick-built Sunday School building of the Bethel Chapel survives as seen in this recent photograph. It was originally hidden behind the corrugated iron chapel of the New Connexion Methodists. (NW)

Below: The Bethel Chapel supported a variety of activities including choirs and a football team: Harts Hill United. Jack Grainger, sitting behind the ball, was the Captain of the team seen here in 1914/15. Soon after this he "joined up" and was killed while on active service. (Winnie Emery's Collection)

of Cochrane's Woodside Ironworks, which provided a suitably dangerous environment in which to play. (It seems that Cochrane's had closed in the early 1920s.)

Alan went to Holly Hall Infant and Junior School and then on to the Senior School in Stourbridge Road. He left at the age of 14 to go and work in the foundry at Hill & Smith. The Second World War had started and he had to take on a man's work as a core-maker. Things improved a year later when he was able to move to Dudley Drop Forging where most of his mates worked. He enjoyed working at the Dudley Drop although his first job was stacking a barrow with hot forgings, with the use of tongs, and then dragging them back to the stores for inspection. Later shift work was introduced, by which time he was on a steel cutting saw cutting up

the billets for the stampers. He became something of a 'general dogsbody' who could stand in wherever necessary when the three-man team of stamper/driver/clipper was incomplete. He also played a vital role in maintaining supplies of coke to each furnace. Coke was in very short supply and a lorry was always waiting at the sidings in Brettell Lane to bring in replenishment. Somehow the furnaces were kept going and war-work continued. When not working he was fire-watching or helping his brother deliver air-raid shelters!

Although such work was a "reserved occupation", by 1944 the Armed Services were in the need of more men and Alan's conscription could no longer be delayed. His boss was told to hire three women - or however many it took to replace Alan, as the Army awaited him. After serving in the Army for three years Alan returned to Harts Hill to take up his father's green-grocery round - but after five years returned to the Dudley Drop. Life in Harts Hill was changing. The slum-clearance of Harts Hill eventually, in the early 1950s, began and the shop lost all of its customers who moved to new council homes in Sledmere or Holly Hall. The shop was eventually compulsorily purchased, and an era came to an end.

Alan has two other enduring memories of Harts Hill. He can vividly recall watching the huge shire horses employed in the Harts Hill Iron Works making their own way up Brick Kiln Street to a field where they enjoyed some 'time off', and he remembers a time in the late 1940s when a film-crew came to his father's yard in Canal Street. It is thought that they were filming scenes for the film called "My Brother Jonathan" from the top of the bonk. The film was released in 1948, and is based on a novel by Francis Brett Young. It is an intriguing thought that this film might preserve some images of bygone Harts Hill.

Left: Houses at 46 and 48 Garratt Street, Harts Hill, in 1954. These houses were awaiting clearance, but the old "viillage" of Harts Hill has been replaced by an industrial estate rather than new housing. (R.Hood)

So little of the old Harts Hill now remains, however this imposing building on the corner of Canal Street and Brick Kiln Street still stands, along with the Bethel Sunday school building. It became the social and sportsclub for employees of Midland Red as it was close to the bus garage - just across the border in Brierley Hill. (Dudley Garage's social club had no premises of their own so this was luxury indeed.) (NW)

Chapter 10
Hall Street to Dixon's Green and Kates Hill

As a male student at Dudley College of Education - at first residing in the new hall of residence in King Edmund Street - I knew there was one fate one should try and avoid - it was a good idea not to fall in love with a girl residing at The Mount - a hall of residence so remote from the college that it might as well have been in Siberia.

Nevertheless, I made a few trips to The Mount and thus became familiar with the world described in this chapter. It is remarkable that Treasure's 1835 map of Dudley shows so clearly the centre of Dudley stretching along its east-west Market Place and High Street axis. At right angles to this two ribbon-like developments show the town's extension following a northerly axis along Wolverhampton street towards Eve Hill and Shaver's End, and along a corresponding southerly line to Dixon's Green. This is the line that connected the world around Eve Hill to the world around The Mount.

The road to Dixon's Green is first called Hall Street, and it left the 'castle-end' of the Market Place and made its way along a narrow thoroughfare towards King Street. There was one short turning off Hall Street, known as New Hall Street. As I was becoming familiar with Dudley in the early 1960s, this area was being cleared to make way for The Churchill Precinct. Old 18th and 19th Century buildings came down to make way for the pedestrianised precinct. This was a major redevelopment of the town, and at the time it seemed a really bold commitment to becoming "modern"… no town would have a future if it didn't have a pedestrian precinct!

The first part of the scheme to be completed was Birdcage Walk - with its aviary, its sculptured frieze by Bainbridge Copnall, and its mural designed by Paul Rudall of the Dudley Grammar School. It enjoyed good proximity to the bus station and excellent views of Castle Hill - later ruined by the building of C & A's store in the car park! 'Phase two' of the development, opened in August 1967, followed the line of Hall Street, and 'phase three' which followed the line of New Hall Street was

Right: Hall Street began at the "castle end" of the market place, and featured these very old buildings. This was the right hand side of the old Hall Street looking towards Dudley Market Place before its demolition in the early 1960s.
On the right is Jack Whitmore's butcher's and poultry shop. Jack came from the Whitmore family who had farmed near Sedgley and had married Gertie Lane, fourth child of Josiah Lane of Eve Hill glassworks fame, in 1911.
(Author's Collection)

Above: Looking down the left hand side of Hall Street from the King Street end. Left to right: Lacey's children's wear (97), Preedy's tobacconist, Dorset's Fruit and Veg, Poole's Fish and Chip Shop (100) and R.P. Maiden's butcher (101), next to an entry. Then Beverley Wines and Carlton House ladies' fashion shop taking us to the corner of New Hall Street, about 1963. (Bill Maiden Colln.)

Below: George Powell, in a white coat, stands outside his shop at 16 Hall Street in the 1940s. His assistant, George Robinson to his right, and the delivery van on the extreme right. George had started retailing in Flood Street but moved to Hall Street when premises became available, although he had to compete with Melia's and Home & Colonial nearby. (Doreen Slater)

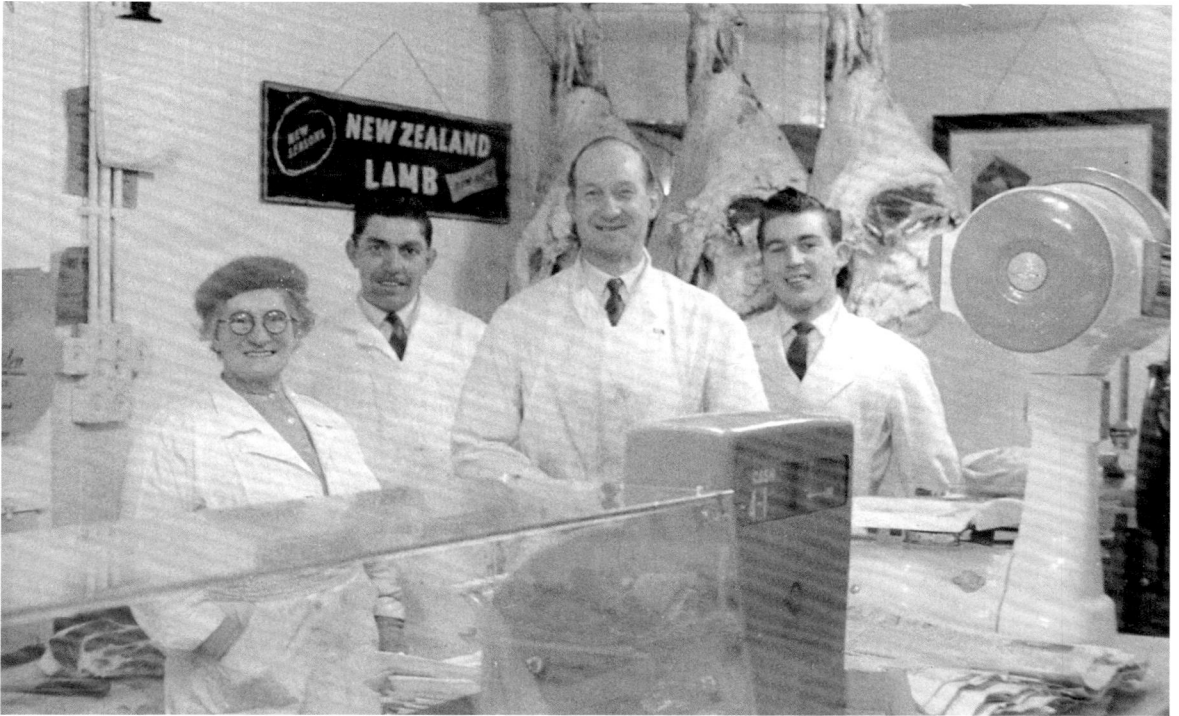

Above: Inside R.P. Maiden's shop at 101 Hall Street. Left to right: Sally Maiden, Rod Walters, Rod Maiden (Sally's son), and unidentified assistant. Rod was the second generation of Maidens to be running this shop, as it had previously been run by his father Dick Maiden. Rod ran the shop until it had to close in 1963. He then briefly ran a shop in Kinver before retiring. (Bill Maiden Colln.)

Below: The Chruchill Precinct and Birdcage Walk replaced the old world of Hall Street. Some of the traders moved from the old to new - eg. Mayo's dress shop seen here in this 1985 picture. Next door is the Birdcage Grill run by Eunice Maiden (Rod Maiden's wife) who took over from her mother Alice Wilcox who had previously run Poole's Fish and Chip shop at 100 Hall Street! (NW)

The Churchill Precinct when new, soon after its 1969 opening. The Churchill Screen was damaged by the wind-tunnel effect of the precinct and was removed. The precinct has since been modernised by being roofed-over. Beatties' store can be seen to the left. (Hilda Walker)

Shops in the new precinct were opened in grand style. Here we see a televsion star coming to open a ladies' hairdresser's shop in the precinct, watched by Michael Coyle, the Precinct Warden, and Hilda Walker who worked at Wimbush's bakery. (Hilda Walker Collection.)

Kendall's fish shop was another of the businesses that made the transition from Hall Street to new premises in the precinct. By then the proprietor was Ron O'Brien and his shop is seen here at 13 Birdcage Walk. Shops selling fresh fish have now become a rarity.
(Hilda Walker Collection)

The Churchill Precinct today (2008) has been refurbished and modernised to keep up with standards set by shopping malls. There is still a number of butchers in and around the precinct. Walter Smith is a Birmingham based firm with a number of branches in the Black Country - some of which, like this one, were acquired at the time of the dissolution of Marsh & Baxter. (NW)

opened by Viscount Cobham on 8th September 1969. It was this final phase that included the Churchill Screen and the Beatties department store. Taking a wider picture, these developments complemented the completion of a pedestrian bridge across King Street linking the precinct to the huge new car parks on the site of the old Flood Street slums - see the chapter on "What's Behind Top Church?"

Wonderful as these developments were, we can now see that they were part of the demise of the 'old Dudley'. By the time they were completed a new Dudley had been created by local government changes, and a new world of retailing was to see off the old world of locally run family businesses.

Planners were doing their best to continue Dudley's 20th Century task of mopping up the problems inherited from the 19th Century, but were also destroying an individuality that might have later stood the town in good stead.

A wonderful night-time picture of Hall Street as it was in 1934 graces the back cover of "Dudley: The Twentieth Century" (Sutton Publishing 1999). This is what the 1960s swept away. The modern world came to an abrupt halt as Hall Street reached King Street, and the top of Birmingham Street. This complicated junction had become an island - created by an earlier "improvement scheme" started in the 1930s with the widening of King Street, and the demolition of a glassworks that enabled Trindle

Road to meet King Street at this point and provide an alternative route through Dudley avoiding the Market Place. Rebuilding the bus station in the 1950s also affected this junction - beyond which Hall Street could continue in the style of "old Dudley" for a few more years.

As I first encountered this "remnant" of Hall Street, it began on the left-hand-side with the premises of Perkes & Co., the seedsmen. On the right were the offices and showroom of the Electricity Board. Both corners became increasingly tatty over the years and the right hand side was demolished in a wave of modernisation that introduced a supermarket to the site. The illustrations show something of the shops of Hall Street as we make our way out of town. The two "landmarks" for me were buildings on opposite sides of the road - on the right the remains of Dudley's Empire Theatre (see later chapter), and, on the left, Hobbs' Fish & Chip Shop.

I discovered the wonders of Hobbs Fish & Chip Shop, at 41 Hall Street, in the early 1980s when I had begun to study vanishing Black Country shops more seriously. I was struck by the amazing tiled interior, but many others will remember it for the legendary quality of its fish and chips when it was run by the Hobbs Family. The story is told in the

next chapter, otherwise we will lose our sense of progressing along Hall Street! Just beyond Hobbs & Son was The Smiling Man public house and shortly beyond that the road ceases to be Hall Street and becomes Waddam's Pool. Today this transition is marked by a bridge that crosses the new Southern By-pass - something I could never have imagined as I trudged back from The Mount in the 1960s. Waddam's Pool may take its name from a sixteenth century Mayor of Dudley, Adam Waddams, but when it was attached to this piece of road is not clear. In the 1880s Hall Street continued much further towards Dixon's Green.

Waddam's Pool also had its interesting features. For me the most significant one was the headquarters of the Dudley Co-operative Society, built in 1929 in fine "moderne" style, and eventually demolished in 1993. It was built on the corner of North Street which contained an interesting Co-op bakery building and the premises of Teddy Gray sweet factory - home of another Dudley legend! On the other corner of North Street there had once been a fine Congregational Church opened on 26th November 1878, known as Christ Church. Its Sunday School hall survived long enough to become an Elim Church in 1956, but all was swept away, and since 1975 a new Salvation Army citadel has occupied the

site. The Salvationists came from their former home in King Street!

On the right of Waddam's Pool is one of Dudley's industrial quarters, starting with the lengthy building used by Goodwin Foster Brown, supplier of flour and food processing products. The land is now empty but has been the centre of controversy when a mosque was about to be built on the site. Beyond this the industrial buildings survive on a huge site where many interesting names could once be encountered like Beans Industries, Alexander Machinery, the National Munitions Factory that eventually became a CWS factory making Co-op electrical goods carrying a "Dudley" brand name, and the elusive Louis Marx. Louis Marx (1896 - 1980) was a successful American toy manufacturer who started toy production in Britain - at this location in Dudley - in 1931. The Marx factory was requisitioned for war work and after the war - in 1948 - the firm moved to Swansea. Much of this industry filled land between Waddam's Pool, Constitution Hill and Blackacre Road, and Bean Road. One of its legacies is the huge red-brick retaining wall still to be seen in Blackacre Road - one of the Wonders of Dudley!

Today's 'Waddam's Pool' eventually becomes Dixon's Green - more or less as it passes Dixon's Green Methodist Church. This church opened in 1870 and survives in a much-rebuilt form. It faces the old community of Kates Hill where further chapels were to be found in Price Street, Brown Street, and an old tin tabernacle at the top of Owen Street. All these have been swept away with much of the rest of the old Kates Hill. It was an area I never really explored in the 1960s and only recently have I tried to understand it. As an outsider I foolishly thought St. John's Road had been the main commercial axis of Kates Hill, but I have since learnt that George Street and Brown Street were much more significant.

To appreciate how much Kates Hill has changed it is a good idea to go back to the turn-of-the-century maps now reproduced by Alan Godfrey. Some street names may have been perpetuated or slightly changed but the over-all street layout and the crowded manner in which it was built up have been totally eradicated. Cross Guns, Pitfield Street, Brown Street, George Street etc. have vanished. St. John's Street, which once continued a very straight line running along Porter Street, Terry Street, right out to Bennett's Hill, has been carved up into little cul-de-sacs with names like Brereton Close and Shirley Road. Grassed open space fills areas that were once densely covered with houses. A tiny stretch of Cromwell Street survives to remind us of Kates Hill's Civil War claim to fame - as the high ground from which Cromwell could train his cannons on Dudley Castle.

At the top of Kates Hill is St. John's Church, sister church to St. James at Eve Hill. Both churches were designed by William Bourne who was later criticised for providing rather "barn-like" structures, however both were "improved" as time went by. The way in which Eve Hill and Kates Hill mirror each other, as Dudley suburbs, make it particularly appropriate that St. John's Kates Hill is sister church to St. James' Eve Hill, or should we say "brother church" as the apostles were brothers. They both start life as "chapels-of-ease" planned in the 1830s as the population of Dudley parish grew. Trustees of the estate of the late Earl of Dudley provided the land and the foundation stones of both churches are

Right: The Dudley Electricity Supply offices on the corner of Hall Street and King Street/Oakeywell Street. These were demolished in the 1970s and replaced with a supermarket but that in turn has been replaced by Cousin's furniture showroom. (W. Boyd)
Left (opposite page): The top of Hall Street as seen from the island at the junction of Birmingham Street, Hall Street and Trindle Road - created in the 1930s to provide a route for through traffic by-passing the High Street. On the right the abandoned Electricity Building is followed by A Moule's paper shop and the Alma pub. On the left Perkes & Co.'s seed shop welcomes travellers to upper Hall Street. (Sam Perks/Doreen Williamson)

Progress up the right hand side of upper Hall Street about 1970. From the Alma pub (seen in previous picture) one came to Phipps' sweet shop, Morris' toy shop, then this derelict shop next door to Fleming's famous faggots and peas shop, seen here awaiting demolition. Next door to the left was Baker's fruit shop.

From Bakers fruit shop one came to John Jeavon's hairdressing shop at 85 Hall Street, followed by an entry. Then came two single storey shops sharing a smart brick portico. The first had been a jewellers that became Brightwell's wallpaper shop and the second was a grocery: Bassingers later Wilda's. The Empire theatre/cinema had two shops within its frontage: Sam Perks' radio shop and Alf Williams (a Gents' outfitters shop).

Looking back down upper Hall Street towards the new precinct about 1970. Alf Williams' menswear shop and Sam Perks radio shop within the Empire building are now boarded up and the building, used for industrial purposes since the Second Wrold War, awaits demolition. Hobbs' Fish and Chip shop is glimpsed on the far right.
(These pictures were taken by Sam Perks of the radio shop, which by then had moved across the road.)

The left hand side of upper Hall Street looking back towards the new precinct about 1970, showing the distinctive sequence of buildings along this stretch.

Coming round the corner occupied by Perkes seed store one came to Theedam's premises - divided into three shops when they departed for the High Street. Sam Perks moved into one of these, having moved out of the Empire. It had once been a corset shop and later became Williams' cycle shop. Arthur Maiden's butchery occupied part of the next three storey building and then there was another low building before reaching Hobbs' shop. (Sam Perks)

Williams' cycle shop in Hall Street is seen here in October 1985. Next door the Halal fruit, veg and meat shop occupies premises that had previously been a shoe shop. It has now (2008) become an Asian fashion shop, in what has become an increasingly run down stretch of Hall Street. (NW)

David, The School of Motoring and Teddy Gray's shops occupy the first three storey building in this part of Hall Street in October 1985, in a view that looks down past Hobbs' to the Co-op building in the distance. Looking back to the picture on page 110, it can be seen that David's shop had previously been Arthur Maiden's butchers shop. The lower shops are probably the remains of the first wave of building along Hall Street, the higher ones added in late

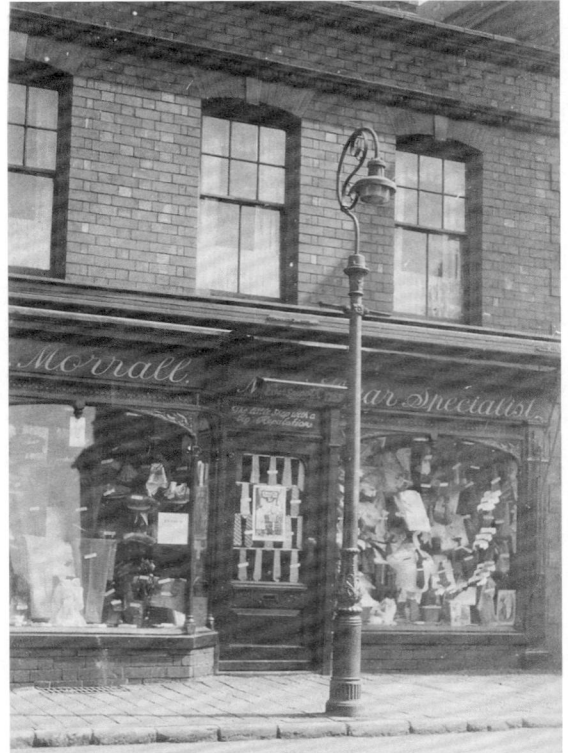

Above left: Hobbs & Sons' fish and chip shop at 41 Hall Street in October 1985, after the Hobbs family had left but with features of the shop still intact. (NW)
Above right: Henry Morrall's gents' outfitters shop at 42 Hall Street, photographed on 1st July 1932. Henry Morrall had worked before the First World War at such a

a shop in Handsworth and after the war was able to fulfil his dream of opening his own shop by taking these premises in Hall Street. He left the shop in the mid thirties, and it was later used by Archibald Rogers then Arthur Ashmore from about 1954 to 1972. (Collection of Tony Morrall)

laid on the same day in October 1838. While St. John's was being constructed the congregation met in a chapel, rented from the non-conformists, in Cawney Bank. This might be the 'unidentified' chapel shown on Treasure's Map.

St. John's and St. James' were consecrated on the same day; 27th July 1840 - the former in the morning, the latter in the afternoon. Both became independent parish churches in 1844. Incredibly, St. John's was led by one minister, Rev. Henry Noot, from then until his death in 1905. Over the years there were enlargements and improvements, a school was added early on, and the church hall on the opposite side of the road arrived much later - opening in 1932. The church came to everyone's attention in 2004 when it was suddenly closed as a result of being declared unsafe. The congregation moved into the church hall, and the fate of the building became the centre of controversy.

St. John's Church has become something of a symbolic landmark - its demise coming at a time when many people feel Dudley has lost its way and demolished a lot of the heritage it could now exploit, and therefore saving St. John's feels like part of a larger matter of saving Dudley itself. The congregation of St. John's may feel happy in its new home in the old Church Hall and maybe saving the church building is matter of persuading the diocese to part with it, setting restoration in motion, and finding a new use for the place. Whether finding a new use can be reconciled with maintaining an interior that can be used for the occasional religious ceremony, accepting that the congregation has crossed the road, is not clear.

Beyond St. John's Church the road crosses the ridge which provides the church with such a magnificent elevated position. As it descends the road passes the old St.John's Church School and runs into Watson's

Above: The premises of Goodwin Foster Brown, Wholesale Grocers, occupied this huge building facing the next stretch of Hall Street.

Right: The Dudley Co-operative Society's head office was strategically placed opposite GFB's building in Waddam's Pool. The Co-op began using premises in this area in about 1902 but this office building was not completed until 1929. It was demolished in 1993. (NW)

Below: Crossing North Street one came to Christchurch Congregational Church, opened in 1878, seen here shorn of its spire, about 1910.

(Ken Rock Colln.)

Green Road. This one-time rural byway started at the top of Cromwell Street and circled the hill, passed Roseland Farm and swung back towards Kates Hill where it was met by Brewery Street. The latter was the north-eastern limit of the old Kates Hill and was home for many years to the Kendrick coach company. The Brewery Street/Watson's Green Road area seemed less remote from the 1930s onwards as the open fields on the northern slope of the ridge - once stretching right down to the Birmingham Road - were built upon, and Watson Green Road was extended so that it looped right round to Claughton Road above the railway tunnel.

Kates Hill was not linked to central Dudley, only St. John's Road. There was also access to Kates Hill via Porter Streer/Terry Street and Claugton Road/Caroline Street. North Street and Firs Street ran at right angles to them and created another enclave of Dudley that still has a distinctive ambience today. The Dudley Southern Bypass has cut them off from the centre of Dudley but the brand new suspension bridge for pedestrians across the bypass shows the planners were aware of this "link" in the town's structure.

Returning to the main road at the bottom of the south-western side of the Kates Hill, Dixon's Green Road quickly comes to Dixon's Green itself. The hamlet took its name from the family who built a local glasshouse. The works, and the family home, were on the lane we now know as Buffery Road.

Treasure's 1835 map notes that the lane led to Halesowen via Netherton. His map also shows that Dixon's Green was quite a hamlet by that time, and like Shavers End, it was a frontier community with a toll gate that stood at the border of Rowley Regis.

By the time the 1900 map, reproduced by Alan Godfrey, was drawn Dixon's Green House had disappeared but The Mount is shown as one of several quite large gentlemen's residences to be found in the Dixon's Green area. Others included Highcliffe, the Woodlands, Springfield House, Cawney Hill House and Cawney Bank House. Further along Oakham Road were Tansley Hill House, Tansley Hill Villa, Oakham Lodge, Wellfield House, and the Hollies. Some of these houses demonstrated their social status by hosting annual fetes and garden parties in the 1890s and 1900s.

One aspect of exploring this area today is to wonder how to accurately apply all these names: Cawney Hill, Kates Hill, Bennett's Hill. Whatever the explanations, ascending these slopes is rewarded with excellent views of Dudley and far beyond. The elevation is explained by the fact that these hills mark the restoration of the ridge that forms the backbone of the Black Country - stretching from Sedgley Beacon to Turner's Hill, Rowley. The centre of Dudley clearly occupies a "saddle" in this ridge, and all this contributes to the interesting views afforded to anyone climbing to the Cawney Hill Reservoir.

Returning to North Street: Teddy Gray's famous sweet factory still produces lettered rock and herbal tablets. An Edward Gray founded the business in 1826, but the present-day business seems to trace its history back to John Gray, the grandfather of the present proprietor. His son started opening shops and selling from market stalls as opposed to being simply a wholesaler. Shops at various times were to be found in Wolverhampton Street, Castle Street, and Hall Street. (NW)

Edward Gray - grandson of John Gray mentioned above at the factory gate at 52 North Street, 2008. At one time the factory belonging to "John Gray &Sons" had been in West Street, but Teddy Gray's has been in North Street since the 1930s.
(Express & Star)

Opposite Teddy Gray's premises we come across this attractive industrial building. For the last twenty three years it has been the home of D.H. Harvey - ornamental gate and fence manufacturers. It was built about 1860 for William Woolley, who lived in the house next door. Over the years it had also been used by Teddy Gray and Arthur Maiden. The character of this section of North Street has been nicely conserved. (NW)

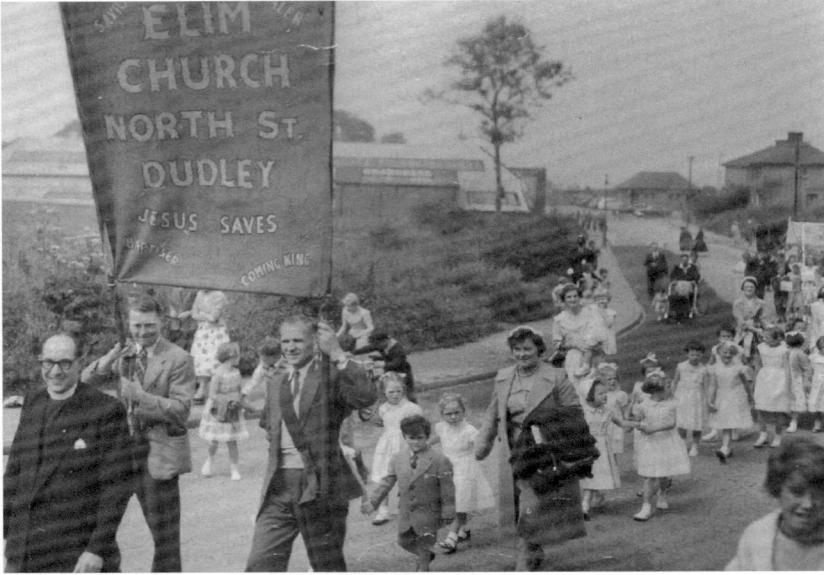

Left: The Elim Church first met in Dudley in 1933 in a room above the Dartmouth Garage, but in 1956 they obtained the use of the old church hall in North Street that had belonged to the Christ Church Congregationalists. Pastor Jones leads the Sunday School children through Kates Hill on a parade in the late 1950s. Neither the Elim nor Congregationalists have survived in North Street, although the Christadelphians have built a large hall nearby in Firs Street.
The corner of North Street and Waddam's Pool is now occupied by a modern Salvation Army citadel. (Bill Webb)

Left: The Salvation Army moved its HQ from the 1932 citadel in King Street to this new hall on the corner of North Street on 29th September 1975. (NW)

Below: The west side of Hall Street - Waddam's Pool and Dixon's Green Road has been the location of much industry. Harpers, the ironfounders, amalgamated with Beans. Then in 1915 their premises were extended to form the National Munitions Factory. In the mid 1930s the Co-operative Wholesale Society used part of the premises, seen here from Constitution Hill at the end of the 1960s. (NW)

Right: The construction of the "National Works" munitions factory in 1915 led to the building of this huge red brick wall in Blackacre Road to retain the built up ground on which the works stood.

On the right is Bean Road leading back up to Dixon's Green Road. This road was once the home of the Blue Coat School but housing now stands on the school's site.

The CWS portion of the works later traded as Allen, and still exists today as part of the Nuttall Group.
(NW)

Above: Dixons Green grew up around the glassworks belonging to John Dixon - clearly marked on Treasure's 1835 map and shown as standing by the Buffery Road which descends from this point down to Baptist End and into Netherton. Here we see The Bush at the beginning of the 20th century, selling Rolinson's ales from Netherton and cared for by longstanding licensee; J. Waish.

Right: In 1937 the old "Bush" was replaced with the pub that still stands on the site today. (Right) Blackacre Road can be seen on the right of The Bush - with Top Church on the skyline. (NW)

117

Above: Hobbs & Sons' Fish & Chip shop at 41 Hall Street, October 1985. The Hobbs family have passed on the business and hot curry and pies are now on offer, but the fabric of the shop has not changed too much. The "new" sign board on the right covers the original word "Restaurant". (NW)

Left: The rear wall of the main part of the shop showing the tiled panels of 'fishy scenes' and the enamelled ceiling. (NW)

Bottom Left: The scene in 2005 when much of the interior had been damaged by invading vandals. The door in this wall led through to the "saloon" where customers could 'eat in'. (NW)

Chapter 11
Hobbs' Fish & Chip Shop

In the previous chapter I made passing reference to Hobbs' fish & chip shop because to have gone into greater detail would have detracted from the attempt to give a more general impression of Hall Street. However, Hobbs' was something of an institution and people came from far and wide to enjoy their legendary chips, and to meet the red-headed family who produced them. It seems appropriate therefore to give an account of this shop in its own chapter.

Joseph Hobbs was born about 1888 and had grown up in the Birmingham Street area of Dudley - a poor and crowded area that disappeared in successive slum clearances and is now obliterated by the existence of the bus station. He was always business-minded and as a lad, tried selling fruit from a barrow. Eventually he was able to buy or lease a small, and relatively uneconomic, fruit shop in Hall Street - a few doors away from the fish and chip shop we are looking at. He talked about being in business for sixty years when retiring in 1976, so may have acquired this shop in 1916. It is not really clear when he moved into 41 Hall Street and set about creating the legendary fish and chip shop, but I would think it must have been about 1926 as that seems to match the date when the Pilkington hand-painted tiles were likely to have been produced. He took this trouble over the interior of his shop because he was fastidious about cleanliness. He later employed two cleaners who scrubbed the tiled walls from floor to ceiling early every morning. In earlier times the premises had been occupied by the Belgrave Laundry.

Joe Hobbs was married to Phoebe in early 1911 and they had three children. Joyce was born in 1916, Reg was born in 1918, and later Derek was born, but he had less to do with the shop. Joyce and Reg both went to Dudley's Grammar Schools, but it seems that their destiny was always clear - they had to become part of the family business. Reg went straight into the shop but Joyce really took over when Phoebe became less able to work. (Joyce took charge when Reg was called-up during the Second

World War.) At one stage the shop employed a staff of sixteen people!

In 1947 Reg Hobbs married Sadie, a girl who had grown up on Kates Hill and who had regularly passed the shop, first on her way to the Intermediate School, and later on her way to work at the offices of Grainger & Smith. Sadie gave up the latter to join her husband in the more exciting life of the chip shop, and is alive today to tell us all about the business.

Joe was determined to make his fish and chips "special". He bought fish that came ashore at Aberdeen and which were sent from there to Birmingham Market. Later Joe had the fish "dropped off" at Dudley Port station, which was more convenient. During the Second World War he was "directed" to

Joe Hobbs - photographed on a firm's outing to Blackpool. (Sadie Hobbs Collection)

obtain Grimsby fish but Joe would have nothing of it. He was similarly particular about flour and always used a special saffron flour that could be obtained locally. This gave the batter and reddish tint - which complemented Reg's auburn hair! They always cooked in dripping supplied by a Dudley firm and never used cooking oil. The fryer was coal-fired and stood against the wall behind the counter - and was kept as "spare" once a more modern fryer was put into the counter. (Chips from a coal-fired fryer are regarded as "special" by connoisseurs.) The potatoes were sourced locally and were always sent back if in any way unsatisfactory - usually having been delivered half a ton at a time.

Work began first thing in the morning. The fish came out of their ice-filled boxes and had to be skinned and boned. Some fish were used to make a display in the shop window. Potatoes in vast numbers had to be peeled etc. By lunch time the shop was busy because workers at the nearby sewing factory (Clifford Williams) had sent in their advance

Left: The 'second generation' of Hobbses:
Left to right: Joyce's husband, Mick Lammas, his son Brian Lammas, Sadie Hobbs carrying her son Gary, Reg Hobbs, his son Robert, and Joyce Roberts.
(Sadie Hobbs Collection)

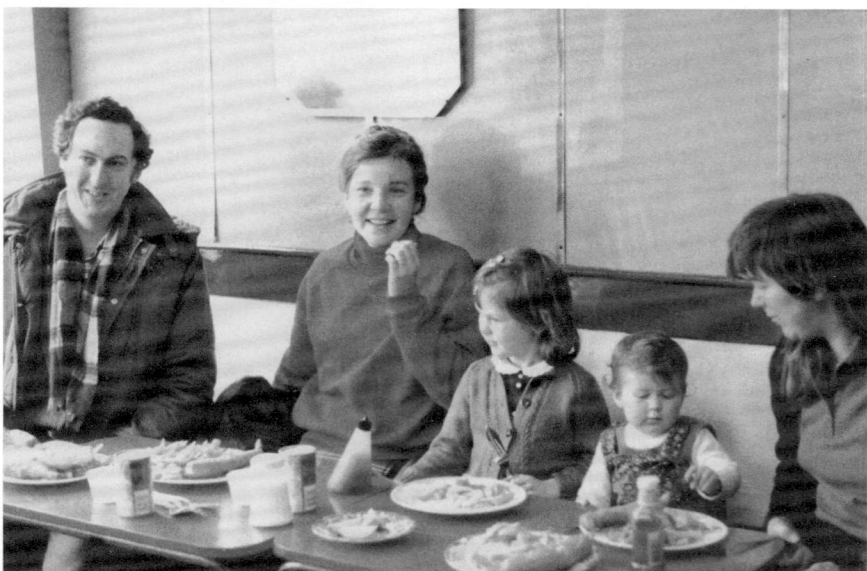

Left: The Williams Family, and guest from Australia, tackling fish and chips at Hobb's Fish & Chip shop in January 1986 - after the Hobbs Family had gone, but still in the vitrolite-lined "Saloon" of the shop as so many people remember it.
(NW)

orders, and girls were coming down to the shop from Hillman's leather factory. The presence of The Empire just across the road guaranteed customers well into the evening. In fact people came from far and wide to purchase their favourite fish and chips.

Joe Hobbs was a hard taskmaster interested in keeping his premises immaculate and ensuring that he sold a top-quality product. He rewarded his staff and family with an annual 'charabanc' trip to the seaside, but generally life was "hard work". Even when the second generation had in effect taken over, Joe would still pop in to see how the business was being run. The Hobbs family only eventually relinquished the business because Joyce was growing older and her husband felt it was time to retire. They sold the business early in 1976, when Joyce was sixty.

The business retained its name but the new proprietor was Greek, and, of course, he broadened the menu. Possibly this would have been sacrilegious to the Hobbs Family as even to this day Sadie Hobbs is quite emphatic when she says, "And we never sold pies". Today the building has gone - and awaits reincarnation at the Black Country Living Museum.

The fate of Hobbs' fish and chip shop had come to a head in 2005, although it is not clear how long the premises had been closed by that time. James Ruston alerted the Express & Star to the state of the building, and the paper's reporter, Heather Loat, produced an illustrated feature on the shop on 1st April, followed by another article on 9th April. The building had been "locally listed" and the Historic Environment Team was trying to persuade the owner, Hekmat Kaveh, to make it more secure and investigate the possibility of preserving the tiled interior. The latter claimed that preservation was too expensive but was willing to give the tiles away to anyone with the skills available to remove them. The Tiles & Architectural Ceramics Society also showed interest, and offered advice.

Right: Just to the extreme left of this picture is the arch which separated the "shop" part of Hobbs & Sons from the saloon in which customers could sit down to enjoy their fish and chips. Next to it is one of the best examples of the tiled panels which were a feature of the shop. The panel is surrounded by a deep green border - matching the dado seen at the foot of the picture. It is also possible to just glimpse the enamelled metal ceiling. (NW)

All this attention possibly made matters worse and vandalism proceeded at a pace. The broken back door did enable me to enter the premises to photograph what remained in 2005, but the prospects remained gloomy. Suddenly when all seemed lost, the Black Country Living Museum was able to intervene. The building was made secure and the process of carefully dismantling it was begun. But life is full of interesting twists. When the building had to be taken down, who should provide the scaffolding to do this? It turned out to be Sadie Hobbs' grandsons!

Hobbs' fish and chips were obviously legendary but were they the best? I have found that Black Country folk are often very loyal to their particular fish and chip shop and thus there may be many contenders to be "the best". I was reminded of this when discussing Hobbs' shop with ex-Kates Hill resident Professor David Hughes. After admitting their quality he added, "They were almost as good as Sofie Webb's on Kates Hill." So, as you can see, once Hobbs' Fish and Chip shop is rebuilt at the Museum there will be much to discuss for years to come.

The corner of Terry Street and St. Johns Road, about 1960. On the corner is Dennis Bloomer's bakery and confectionery, and on the extreme right is The Fir Tree. (Dudley Archives & Local History Centre)

Below: The Fir Tree - St. John's Road, in March 1977. The shop on the left had been Richardson's fruit shop. There as now apartments at this location. (Keith Hodgkins)

Chapter 12

A Portrait of Kates Hill

As I have said earlier, Kates Hill has been an area of Dudley that was relatively unknown to me. It was being "cleared" at the time I was beginning to explore Dudley, and was rather "off my beat" as my life had first been centred on Eve Hill, and then Holly Hall. It is, of course, possible to discover an area retrospectively by talking to the people who once lived there. This is what I have had to do.

Kates Hill soon reveals itself as a quite distinct self-contained area. It grew quite quickly from the 1820s onwards and hosted miners and nailers and workers in the developing metal trades. By the twentieth century there were folks on Kates Hill who could feel they had been there for at least three generations, but the area's growth meant there was a steady stream of incomers, and some movement of families between Kates Hill and other parts of Dudley. The area's "rough" reputation did not take account of the mixture of people to be found on Kates Hill, but social class bounderies were sometimes reflected in geographical boundaries. Dixon's Green Road is a good example of that - the western side of the road was seen as distinctly more "respectable" and with the creation of Buffery Park with its band stand and tennis courts, its middle class credentials seemed sealed. The fact that some local Methodists felt dissatisfied with their membership of the Dixon's Green Chapel is reflected in the fact that they broke away and firmly established themselves in the heart of Kates Hill. Henry Rollason left Dixon's Green with twelve followers who became the trustees of his "independent" mission in Price Street where they had to rebuild a stable and yard to meet their purposes. It seems in later times that the Price Street Mission folk felt more at ease with the Anglicans at St. John's than with the folks at the Bethel who may have seemed "too close" to the folks at Dixon's Green!

The degree to which Kates Hill could seem self-contained is reflected in the range of services available. Church and Chapel folk were both well served, and there was no shortage of public houses! When it came to retail needs Kates Hill had "everything" including a post office on the corner of Terry Street and St. John's Road, and the Co-op in George Street. Education was available at two schools - the church school by St. John's, and the "Council Primary" - between whom there was some rivalry. The "Council Primary" prided itself as the 20th century progressed with the number of scholars who progressed to Dudley's Grammar Schools. Such successful pupils were likely, however, to eventually move away from Kates Hill. One of Kates Hill's most famous escapees was James Whale who was born at 41 Brewery Street on 21st July 1889 and went on to become a Hollywood film director.

Entertainment was available not far way in Dudley, but in the nineteenth century there had been a Kates Hill Wake - probably held on ground at the top of Cross Guns. At the very beginning of the twentieth century Kates Hill may have produced its own local showman in the shape of Jack Hayes who seems to have travelled a bioscope show from a base in Kates Hill. (See the chapter on "Entertainment")

Because houses in some parts of Kates Hill were of poor early nineteenth century construction it was targeted by the slum clearance programmes that began in the 1930s. This left open spaces and demolition sites for post-war children to explore and exploit. It also meant that by the 1960s this process had resumed and gained momentum, thus destroying a Kates Hill that had taken a century and a half to develop.

The Kates Hill Hairdresser at 10 Brown Street, 1910. People alive today remember Thomas Holyhead as the barber of Brown Street between the wars.
(Dudley Archives & Local History Centre)

Above: Brown Street, Kates Hill, looking up towards St.John's Road at the junction of Caroline Street. Note the Four Ways Inn on the left, followed by a grocery shop, then Aldridge's crockery shop, Lacey's fancy work and embroidery, then Aldridges' wallpaper shop. 1959.

Below: The top portion of Cross Guns Street, Kates Hill, opposite the wasteground where the wake might once have been held. This picture "continues" on the opposite page.

(Above: Dudley Archives, Below: Prof. David Hughes)

Above: George Street, Kate's Hill. Note the Dudley Co-op Society's grocery on the left, followed by their greengroccery and butchery departments. We are looking up towards the lower end of Cromwell Street.
(Dudley Archives)

The continuation of Cross Guns Street, looking down towards Dixon's Green Road. The Cross Guns pub was on the far corner, and survived into the late 1970s, after the rest of the buildings in the street had been demolished.
(Prof. David Hughes)

Above: St. John's Church, Kates Hill seen from St. John's Road. From the other side, this church occupies a "landmark position" and can be seen from Castle Gate. The foundation stone was laid in October1838 and construction was completed ready for the consecration on 27th July 1840. In that year the vicar, the Rev. Noot was appointed and he served Kates Hill for 65 years! (NW)

Below: St. John's Church, Kates Hill: the interior. In 2004 the structure of the church was suddenly deemed unsafe and the building has been closed ever since. The congregation moved into the Church Hall (of 1932 vintage) and the future of the church building has become a matter of great controversy. A "preservation group" was formed in 2007. (Save St. John's Church Group)

Right: A meeting in St. John's Church Hall held on 27th November 2007 was an opportunity for all parties to express their views regarding the future of St. John's Church. Seated: Rev. David George, Priest in Charge at St. John's, Arch-Deacon Fred Trethewey, Brian Wentworth, church warden and John Dentith representing the diocese - listening to local Councillor Shaukat Ali appealing to all sides to work together. The Black Country Society and the Birmigham historian Carl Chinn, plus many others, have come forward to support the preservationists. (NW)

Right: St John's Church School survives in private ownership. (NW)

Below: In March 1977 the top of Kates Hill looked like a vast building site as work progressed on new houses that now spread across the top of the hill in a maze-like new pattern of streets. Note St. John's Church and Dudley Castle beyond. (Keith

Left: Looking along Price Street, with St. John's on the horizon, one can just make out the entrance to the Price Street Mission on the right - next door to Edgar Westley's brass foundry! Picture taken in 1959. (Dudley Archives)

Below: The 1966 Sunday School Anniversary inside the Price Street Mission, Kate's Hill. To the left of the banner is Leonard Edmunds the Sunday School teacher who taught the children the anniversary words and music, and on the right is Reg Hadley, School Secretary. (Prof. David Hughes)

The Bethel "Independent Methodist" Chapel in Kates Hill was on the corner of Brown Street and High Street. It was opened in 1867 and almost lasted a century! Here we see the Sunday School Anniversary of 9th May 1937. (Doreen Williamson

Right: The front elevation and side of Dixon's Green Methodist Church tell two different stories: The side belongs to the original chapel of 1869/70, while the front "extension" is a modern addition dating from 1950. The interior has also been modernised. The chapel has absorbed members of the congregations of Price Street, the Bethel and Burnt Tree.
(NW)

Right: Children at Kates Hill Council School completing some folk dancing - taught and photographed by Miss Allbut. Miss Allbut taught the top class and was well known for ability at getting pupils to Grammar School.

The school was at the junction of St.John's Street and Owen Street., and has since been replaced by a more modern school. (From the collection of Bill Goodman.)

Right: Staff at Kates Hill Junior School, as it was known after the War, in 1948. Left to right: Mr. Whitehouse, Ron Willetts, Mr. Probst and Dick Unsworth.
Seated: Margaret Addis, Miss Chandler, Sid Carter (The Head Master, whose home was in Aston Road) Pru Allbut, and Jessamy Weston.
(From the Collection of Margaret Pearce.)

Above: A pageant presented by Kates Hill Council School about 1935. (Prof. David Hughes, whose mother can be identified, right hand side of second row.)

It is questionable how far "Kates Hill" extends 'over the bonk'. The nineteenth century boundary seems to have been Watson's Green Road, so here we pause at The Ivy House, in 'rebuilt form' on the corner of Brewery Street and Watson's Green Road in the late 1940s as driver Albert Watts, of Bridgewater Crescent (extreme left) poses with passengers before a trip. (Val Davies Colln.)

Chapter 13
Town Centre Pictorial

Dudley has a very well defined and relatively compact town centre stretching from St. Edmund's Church to St. Thomas' Church via Castle Street, Market Place and High Street. The streets on either flank of this axis also contribute to the town centre although each flank has a different character. King Street had a life of its own, changed by its widening at various times, and now of much reduced significance. On the other hand, the streets on the other side of the central axis seem to enjoy a very different life and contain several buildings with good architectural credentials should Dudley eventually wish to exploit its central built environment.

In the midst of it all is Dudley's market place - surely a symbol of the commercial importance to which the town aspired. Market places in general have had a difficult time since the 1960s, and Dudley's has undergone a number of changes. Something "bold" has to happen to take the town centre forward into the twentyfirst century.

Above: Castle, Church and Market Place in the 1950s.
Below: St. Edmund's Church and Castle Street about 1910 looking towards the Market Place. The Earl of Dudley's statue no longer surveys such a peaceful scene but some of the buildings on the right have been preserved.
(Both pictures from Ken Rock Collection)

The interior of St. Edmund's Church, photographed in August 2007. The original church on this site was destroyed in 1646 and work on this one did not begin until 1724. There were alterations and renovations in 1814, 1849, 1864 and 1876.
The Parish of Dudley was divided in 1844 when St. Thomas', St. Edmund's, St. John's and St. James' all became separate parishes. (NW)

A Raphael Tuck "photochrome" postcard view of the Castle end of the Market Place about 1905. Note the old Hen & Chickens pub, replaced in the 1930s, on the left and the shop replaced by Burtons, on the corner of Hall Street, on the right. (From the postcard collection of Bob Jackson)

A "Valentines" postcard of Dudley Market Place about 1962. Littlewoods, Woolworths and Marks & Spencer have arrived on the far side of the market. British Home Stores opened on the right hand side. In the distance the outline of the Dudley Arms still forms the skyline. Some 'more brutal' 1960s buildings are just creeping in on the extreme left. (From postcard collections of Keith Hodkins and Ken Rock.)

Various decades are represented in this view of the western end of the Market Place. The Countess of Dudley's Drinking Fountain was opened in 1867. Woolworths was rebuilt with this frontage at the end of 1929 in the style of the time and Littlewoods has gone for a post 1960s makeover.
(NW)

At one time the Maypole Dairy had a branch right next to Woolworths at 35 Market Place. The chap in the doorway is Dennis Ball who later died in Java as a PoW during the Second World War.
(Viv Turner Collection)

The Dudley Arms Hotel was a significant Georgian addition to Dudley's townscape and replaced an earlier inn called The Rose and Crown in 1786. It provided a "club-like" facility for Dudley's gentry and a meeting place for the Town Commissioners.
The Frontage became increasingly corrupted by the infringement of shops etc., and the hotel was demolished in 1968 to provide room for Marks & Spencer to expand. (It was intended that the coat of arms should be preserved by the Black Country Museum..) This picture is said to have been taken in 1886.
(Les Bywater Collection)

Left: Wimbush's sold bread and cakes from their shop overlooking the market, a few doors away from British Home Stores, until moving to 67 Birdcage Walk and then 70 Churchill Precinct. Left to right: Margaret Westwood, Margaret Andrews, Manageress Hilda Walker, who worked for Wimbush's for 49 years, Janet ?, and Flossie Edwards. (Hilda Walker)

Below: A branch of the Alliance & Leicester Building Society moved to the Market Place on 13th. February 1992. Roger Hodson, manager, surrounded by Carol, Helen, Jane, Michelle, Kay, Jill, Karen and Mala. (Roger Hodson)

High Street, Dudley.

Above left: Beyond the recent Duncan Edwards statue is the Market Place facade of the Fountain Arcade of 1925, and the offices of The Dudley & District Building Society, founded by Doylah Tanfield in 1862. (NW)

Above right: J. Bunce's drapery and Bunny's toyshop occupied the ground floor of this Georgian building in High Street, photographed in 1970 before being swept away to make way for the Trident Centre. (NW)

Lower opposite page: Traditional Market-trader at work! A crock trader in mid spiel occupies a pitch in the Market Place on 10th August 1999 - in "National Market Week".

Above right: An Edwardian postcard view of Dudley High Street (The Milton Series) looking towards Top church. On the right: Freeman, Hardy & Willis, on the corner of Wolverhampton Street, followed by Lipton's, then Grey's, then Bunney's, then Bunce's. (A postcard in the collection of Dorothy Nicklin.)

Right: Evans & Maiden advertising their business at 171 High Street in 1905. The partnership was dissolved four years later, but Tom Maiden eventually re-appeared at 191 High Street in partnership with Hilda Whitmore, his sister. (Bill Maiden)

Above: Messrs. Evans & Maiden, at 171 High Street, opposite Top Church, possibly in 1894. William Maiden stands in the doorway with his son Tom. The latter married Anne Jewkes in 1917 - see page18, and Maidens also married Whitmores....This picture shows ox hearts, ox heads and suckling pigs displayed in a way quite uknown to us today. The business was dissolved in 1913.
(Bill Maiden's Collection)

Below: John Fleming's shop at 73 High Street was next door to F. W. Cook's large premises. The latter was a very old established Dudley drapery business going back to Samuel Cook's first shop of 1819. (He became a radical Chartist - which is 'another story'...) Like many chemists, John Fleming moved into photography, and later into books.
(The late Tony Walker)

Chapter 14
Transport

When I arrived in Dudley in the Autumn of 1962 I was already a committed transport enthusiast. It might be expected, therefore, that I took out my camera to record the fascinating details of the transport scene I discovered in Dudley, but once again my priorities as an eighteen-year-old let me down, plus my naivety about what was going to last and what was going to vanish. Coming from London I was naturally delighted to meet 'Midland Red' for the first time and to travel on the No.58 green and primrose trolleybuses supplied by Wolverhampton Corporation for the Dudley route. Further "colour" was encountered at the Fisher Street bus station by the blue buses from Walsall, plus the buses in West Bromwich and Birmingham colours on the 74 service.

Luckily there were bus and trolleybus enthusiasts out there in the 1960s taking photographs and recording information. Their pictures remind us not only of the vehicles and services, but often take the from of very evocative street scenes - some of which have been featured in this book. Other forms of transport often can be glimpsed in such pictures, reminding us that now we can also look back at delivery vehicles, milk floats, lorries, ambulances, police cars, etc... and feel nostalgic about them, and crave to see local examples.

Dudley's railway station was an amazing place and already seemed very neglected and decrepit. The Wolverhampton - Stourbridge services had just ceased but there were three services still running: to Birmingham via Great Bridge, to Walsall, and along the "Bumble Hole" line to Old Hill. If I had read the small print in the timetable more closely I would have also noticed that the last vestiges of the "dodger" service to Dudley Port could also have been experienced. I suppose one reason for feeling a bit "low key" about these rail journeys at the time was that most trains were the ubiquitous green diesel multiple units. Now I look back on such trains as affording fabulous front seat views of the railway system and the surrounding Black Country, but then they seemed too commonplace and also represented the demise of "steam".

My attention therefore turned towards the train service from Dudley to Old Hill. The service was not helpful as it only ran during morning and evening "rush hour" during the week. However, on Saturdays there was a mid-day return trip available.

Below: Ex GWR 0-6-0PT no. 6434 stands in the "Western" side of Dudley Station having just arrived with the 7.00.pm service from Old Hill, over the 'Bumble Hole Line' on the penultimate day of operation: 12th June 1964. (George Bennett)

Left: Ex GWR 2-6-2T No. 4114 takes the 17.35.pm Snow Hill - Brettell Lane train out of the "Midland" side of Dudley Station. (Trains arriving from Birmingham had to use this side of the station - all part of the station's complicated life as a frontier between companies and then regions.) Note that access to this side of the station was from Tipton Road, and the "overbridge" housing the booking offices led across to the "Western" side with access from Station Drive on the edge of Castle Hill.
(George Bennett)

Left: Ex LMS 2-6-0 no. 46490 with a short parcels train on 17th May 1963. The Tipton Road is on the right, and where it met Birmingham Road there was once a tram shed overlooking the station. Note how St. John's Church in Kates Hill occupies the horizon. Trees have now grown which obscure it during the Summer. (A Peter Shoesmith photo in the author's collection)

Left: One after one of Dudley's rail passenger services were withdrawn as the mid 1960s progressed and the station - never a very bright place - grew ever more dismal. When this picture was taken on 20th January 1967 demolition of the station was well underway although goods traffic had a future for a while. Geoffrey Jackson is the shunter seen with signal man Bill Hart. Dudley South box was one of three signal boxes at Dudley station.
(Bob Jackson Collection)

Dudley Freightliner Depot opened on the site of the former station on 6th. November 1967, five months after the new signal box on the right. The depot, seen here in early 1980s, closed on 29th. September 1986 but the tracks on the right remained open for freight traffic between Bescot and Stourbridge Junction until 19th. March 1993. On that day Dudley ceased to be on the railway network entirely. The proposed "Metro" system would have to cross this site to make its way into Dudley. (Brian Robbins)

This, and usually one of the evening trains, was usually a steam train. The train was in the grand branch line tradition of being a small GWR pannier tank plus one coach - sometimes operated on a "push-pull" basis, sometimes not. I explored the potential of this railway - the "Bumble Hole Line" - as much as I could and recorded what I saw on a minimal amount of 8mm cine film, but only took one or two photographs as closure took place in June 1964. Likewise, I was fascinated by the 'goods only' branch from just south of Baptist End Halt down to the goods depot and canal transhipment facility at Netherton (Withymoor Basin). Like others I viewed all this from the footbridge thoughtfully provided at the Northfield Road Level Crossing - but only allowed myself to take one photograph!

I made farewell trips on the trains to Birmingham and to Walsall but took no photos, nor lavished any precious cine film upon them. I will have to live with my guilt and regrets for the rest of my life! The truth is that it took me a long time to develop a basic comprehension of the Black Country's complex railway network, and to appreciate what I was missing. It was not until the 1980s that I began to "catch up" - resulting in two books about Wolverhampton's railways, produced in partnership with Simon Dewey, then two books about the Black Country system, and then "The Railways of Dudley" which came out as late as 1994. Meanwhile I had also chronicled the history of the Wombourne line, and worked with Michael Hale on doing the same for the Dudley-Halesowen line, which, in part, was

about the late lamented Bumble Hole line. (By Rail to Halesowen, Hale & Williams, 1974)

Even in the early 1980s it was possible to believe that Dudley's Freightliner Depot might live forever, or that trains would continue to make their way up to the trading estate at Pensnett. I should have heeded what had gone before and understood that "transport" (like entertainment and retailing) is the most obvious manifestation of the impermanence of all things. Dudley's remaining presence on the railway system ebbed away and few people turned out on 19th March 1993 to see the last freight trains pass through the town. Since that time we have been teased with stories that the line might re-open, or that the route might be used by an extension to the Metro system.

Dudley's railway history does not lack interest. It featured in the 'gauge-war' of the mid-nineteenth century, it became a frontier between two major systems characterised by the initials GWR and LMS. The station itself suffered at least one major fire and was continually the subject of complaint by Dudley citizens who never forgave it for being slightly inaccessible in the first place. The services, both passenger and freight, were interesting. Yet all these things do not add up to the whole story of rail transport in Dudley! Dudley also had some industrial systems, the miniature railway in Dudley Zoo, and the Earl of Dudley's railway system also ran into the borough - most noticeably with a branch to Wellington Road.

Just as I arrived in Dudley in 1962 the closure of Dudley Canal Tunnel was announced. This was formalised by placing a heavy beam across the entrance to the tunnel at Parkhead. We were shown this on one of our early tours of Dudley organised by Jack Aldiss. Parkhead, of course, had everything! Three canals met at this point - more or less beneath the arches of a railway viaduct. Rumours circulated about the existence of a Boulton & Watt steam engine in a nearby building. We were being inducted in industrial archeaology probably before the term had been invented. Parkhead became a place to return again and again, especially after moving to Holly Hall. And from Parkhead it was possible to follow towpaths to all parts of the Black Country, even passing through the famous Netherton Tunnel if necessary.

Vic Smallshire was one of the local people who appeared from nowhere to help me explore Dudley and the Black Country - taking me into subterranean worlds beneath the Wren's Nest and Castle Hill. The next thing I knew was that Vic was taking part in the campaign to re-open the tunnel - and ultimately taking steps to assure its future. So - despite the lack of real commercial traffic - it was a good time to discover the canals and it was exciting to take part in the "Dudley Digs" both at Parkhead and at the Black Country Museum site. It was also a great day when the Dudley Canal Tunnel reopened on 21st April 1973, although I had been taking trips through the tunnel since 1965.

At first Dudley, as a result of its hill-top location, would not seem a good place to find canals. Perhaps that is why it was a tunnel that reinvigorated everyone's interest in canals. However, Dudley's boundary included Netherton - a land where the canals came into their own with places like Windmill End, Lodge Farm - and, over towards Woodside, the mystery of the Two Locks Line. Once the search was underway for a location for a Black Country Museum, it was inevitable that a site that could be linked to canal history was likely to be favoured.

The worlds of railways and canals come together at Parkhead, where the canals and the railways both climb towards Dudley and then plunge into tunnels to come out on the eastern side of the ridge. Left: 47310 crosses the Parkhead Viaduct on tis way from Brierley Hill Steel Terminal to Bescot on 15th March 1993 - three days before closure of the line. In the foreground the Dudley No.1 Canal, having left the tunnel, descends through locks to make its way westwards. (NW)

Left: The Netherton Canal Tunnel of 1858 was built to relieve congestion in the Dudley Tunnel of 1792. On 20th August 2008 the Netherton Tunnel celebrated its 150th birthday and here we see the Mayor of Sandwell trying to cut the ribbon on leaving the tunnel, assisted by the Deputy Mayor of Dudley, Pat Martin. (Express & Star)

The steam trams provided the first mechanised public transport on the roads of Dudley. Steam trams linked Dudley to Wolverhampton via Sedgley, to Wednesbury, Birmingham, and out westwards to Stourbridge. Eventually tramways were electrified and the last steam tram ran from Dudley Station to Wednesbury on 15th June 1904. This picture was taken at Tipton Road a few days before that. (Author's Collection)

Below: Dudley Opera House and Castle Hill form a backdrop to this view of the tram terminus and junction of routes, in early 1920s. The entrance to the tram depot was just behind the booking office on the right. (Eric Bytheway Collection)

The railway bridge at the foot of Castle Hill and the start of the Birmingham Road was a major tram interchange point. Tram passengers from Birmingham and Wednesbury would find their journeys terminated here and would have to walk a few yards towards Dudley to catch the single deck cars working through the town and heading west.

Right: Here we see car no. 15 of the Dudley & Stourbridge Co.'s fleet, standing on the bridge by the Station Hotel (mark 1 version) in about 1900. (Author's Collection)

Some tram services turned round by the fountain in Dudley Market Place - eg. the service to Netherton, Old Hill and Cradley Heath. Stourbridge-bound trams usually started from the Station Hotel. Services on the Wolverhampton line started from the Wolverhampton Street Post Office. (Author's Collection)

The tramway from Wolverhampton to Dudley had been horse-worked, then steam-worked and then electrified! The process of converting from electric tram operation to a trolleybus service was long and complicated and conversion was not complete until July 1927. The new service continued from the Post Office down Priory Street and swung round into a terminus in Stone Street - now a town square! Here we see vehicle no.490 pausing to unload passengers outside the papershop. The Saracen's Head is in the back-ground. (May 1960) (Douglas F. Parker)

Left: Trolleybuses queue up at the Stone Street terminus and wait to return to Wolverhampton on route 58. Note the weighbridge and the buiding next to the trolleybus - Dudley's first fire station. The last trolleybuses ran from here on 5th March 1967. (Michael Dryhurst)

Above: Dudley's Mayor, Councillor Arthur Silcox, opened Phase 1 of Dudley's new bus station on 27th September 1952. Slums in the Birmingham Street area had been cleared and the new bus station slowly took shape. (BCS Collection)

Right: Services like the No.74 were operated by Birmingham Corporation and could now at last serve the centre of Dudley. A Leyland PD2 of 1949 vintage, 2136, in blue and cream livery stands in Birmingham Street about 1960. St. Edmund's School can be seen to the left.
(Michael Dryhurst)

Right: A West Bromwich Corporation bus, no.158, in cream and two shades of blue, stops at the same spot. The vehicle is a Daimler CVG6 built in 1952.
A sloping bus station may not have been a good idea! After many changes the present bus station follows the more horizontal axis of Fisher Street.
(Michael Dryhurst)

143

Pictures of buses often contain interesting backgrounds, particularly when the location of the bus station has been carved out of an existing townscape.
Left: Midland Red No.3562, built in Wolverhampton by Guy, and garaged at Dudley, stands in the bus park that was once part of Porters Field. St. Joseph's Catholic School forms the background. Picture taken in October 1956.
(Douglas Parker)

In 1969 the West Midlands Passenger Transport Executive took over some bus networks of the area, and the 'standard' blue and cream livery replaced the variety once seen in Dudley. Midland Red made it into the WMPTE via the National Bus Company (1970 -73).

Centre: An ex Midland Red Daimler Fleetliner takes on the B87 service - a number and route inherited from tramway days. The Express & Star recently described Cavendish House as a "landmark building"; another term would be "eye-sore"! (R. Hood)

Left; West Midlands no. 2703 in Black Country Heritage livery in the re-aligned bus station in June 1987 while on the B87 service. Since "Deregulation" we have seen vehicles in variety of liveries back in Dudley, but access to and from the bus station is still a problem..
(Roger Hodson).

Above: Dudley Bus Garage was opened by the Midland Red company on 2nd August 1929 and was built above a number of mine shafts. The garage could stable up to 50 vehicles and handsome offices adjoined. Behind was a large yard. Many buses turned round at the island in the foreground adding to traffic chaos at this point. (Dudley Archives & Local History Centre)

Right: West Midlands no. 6325 passes through the 'washer' in the yard behind Dudley Bus Garage on 17th March 1988. Note the destination blind suggests there is such a place as "Derby End". (Roger Hodson)

Below: Last day at Dudley Bus Garage! The garage closed on 28th August 1993 and was demolished to make way for the Castle Gate Island and the Dudley Southern Bypass. Mark Priest hung a banner across the last two buses to leave the garage, 6660 and 2842. (Roger Hodson)

A town like Dudley would have been home to several coach operators in the past, and in Dudley's case the most famous was Kendrick's Coaches - originally based at Brewery Street in Kates Hill. Later the firm acquired premises for garaging coaches and carrying out repairs at Princes End outside Dudley.

Above: KFD 9, A Burlingham bodied Crossley SD42 of 1949 vintage looks very smart in the grey and cream livery of the company. It is posed here outside the entrance to Burton Road Hospital (see page 58). The vehicle was in Kendrick's fleet until 1960.

Left: After the Second World War Kendrick's Coaches opened offices in a shop at no. 8 Wolverhampton Street. Inside the shop Margaret Davies and Cynthia Griffin wait for customers. Kendrick's offered a full range of services from day trips to regular contract works' services such as those taking Black Country workers to firms like Cadbury's. (All pictures from Bernice Giles' Collection)

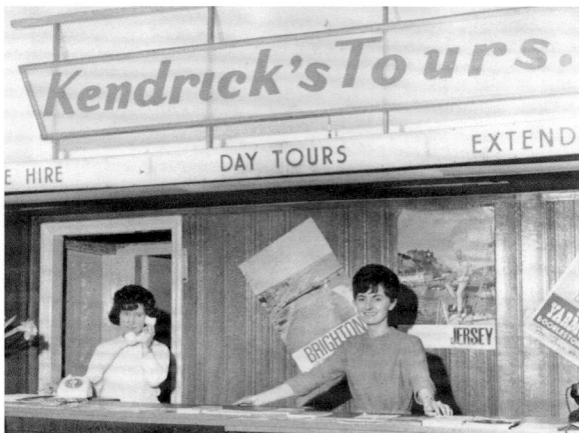

Chapter 15
Entertainment

I recall once attending an interview and being asked, "When you first arrive in a new town, where would you first want to visit: a café, a cinema or a museum?" Despite a strong sense that I was suppose to show my thirst for academic knowledge by saying that I would rush to the museum, I felt compelled to opt for the café, knowing that I would make for the cinema as soon as I had enjoyed a cup of tea! Social interaction, refreshment and entertainment all seemed more interesting than gazing at glass display cases full of dusty objects.

Museums may have become more exciting since those far-off days of the 1960s, but I remember coming to Dudley and becoming familiar with the Odeon and the Plaza long before wondering what delights might exist in the Brooke-Robinson Museum! The descent of Castle Hill on a Friday night inevitably meant a visit to the cinema. It was also a descent into a world of 1930s architectural interest with Zoo entrance, Plaza, Odeon and Hippodrome. However, my mind was focussed on what was to be seen on the screen, and not the bricks and mortar. After all, I had grown up in a world, which included Film Societies and the international range of film that could be seen in London. Ironically, it was my pursuit of more interesting films that led me to discover that places of entertainment were of interest in their own right - possibly more interesting than the entertainment itself!

My desire to see interesting films led in two directions. Firstly it took me off on the No.58 trolleybus to Wolverhampton where there was a thriving film society, in which I later played an active part. It also took me on motorcycle journeys to obscure cinemas who were showing a non-mainstream product as a result of the cinema industry's restrictive practices and "barring" arrangements. Thus I went to The Penn cinema, the Imperial Walsall, the Clifton, Wolverhampton and the Rex, Blackheath. Sometimes I would leave my crash helmet at the box office and on retrieving it would be met by the manager who would want to know where I had come from? When I replied, "Dudley", in my London accent, he would normally say that no-one had ever come to his cinema before from so far away. Sometime this was followed by an invitation to inspect the premises!

Thus it was that one night in 1966 I came out of the Alexandra Cinema in Lower Gornal to be offered the posters as the manager removed them from their display frames. He was absolutely amazed that anyone from outside Lower Gornal had come to his humble cinema. (I had walked from Pensnett Road!) Two things happened. First of all, I suddenly realised that the building and the strange business of presenting entertainment were incredibly interesting, and secondly I resolved to return. When I did so I found the cinema had closed. Somewhere in

Dudley's Odeon on Castle Hill was built at the height of Oscar Deutsch's cinema building career, and was designed by the Harry Weedon Partnership. It was opened on 28th. July 1937 by the Mayor, Alderman Hillman. It was Dudleys' largest cinema, and the last to be built within the old Borough bounderies. The author was present when it closed on 22nd February 1975. (This picture comes from the collection of one of the cinema's managers: The late Joe Alexander.)

Dudley's Odeon was eventually sold to the Jehovah's Witnesses for use as a conference hall. They have worked on the restoration and improvement of the building ever since, possibly making it one of the most cared-for buildings in Dudley, considering it was an empty shell in poor condition when they moved in. This picture was taken in 2000 at one of their "open days." Now we need someone to exercise the same care of the Hippodrome! (NW)

my brain an impulse to record cinema history stirred. Years later, in 1980, as I met the demolition gang working in the Colosseum, Dudley Road, Wolverhampton I knew that I had to start the task that resulted in the production of my book, "Cinemas of the Black Country".

But back to Dudley in the early 1960s and the walk down Castle Hill. On my left was the solid might of the Dudley Hippodrome. Most of the time it was presenting girl shows with names like "Strip, Strip Ahoy - the Great Navel Review" and "Nudes of the World". Stupidly I acted with the disdain well rehearsed by eighteen-year-olds. I should have dashed in and enjoyed not only the shows - which are now part of show-biz history, but also the wonder of that theatre: a major provincial class "A" theatre built in 1938 against all the trends, a theatre with a history of shows that sound like the chapters of a history of post-war British "Variety" theatre. Once the Hippodrome had closed, or "faded away", I realised the folly of my ways.

Since then I have visited the Hippodrome many times, delved into its history, collected material relating to it, and the Kennedy family who owned it, and wished many times that someone would recognise its value to Dudley. Delving into the history of one theatre leads on to other things. The Hippodrome was preceded by the Dudley Opera House and another line of enquiry opens up. The man who brought an Opera House to Dudley - John

Maurice Clement - had previously operated in the Colosseum Theatre, round the corner in Trindle Road. In no time the researcher is lost in the lime-lit world of theatre history and the topic becomes vast.

Up in Hall Street was Dudley's "other" theatre: The Empire. Once again the story is complicated and there are "predecessors" to be accounted for as that part of Dudley has quite an entertainment history going back into the world of the nineteenth century circus. From there it is a small step into the world of "travelling entertainment" - a topic so obscure that it is seldom given much space in local histories.

In this case we have to be grateful to someone who attended the opening of the new Dudley Opera House in 1899 on behalf of The Dudley Herald and not only described that event, but went on to look back at the town's theatrical past. The writer, simply identified by the initials "T.B.", goes back to his memories of 1846, ..."a year I remember well",... and goes on to describe how Dudley folk at that time had to travel into Birmingham to see a theatrical performance. He tells us that the trip involved having a tripe supper in the Bull Ring, and then going to The Theatre Royal in New Street, and then returning to Dudley on Attwood's coach which reached the Dudley Arms Hotel by about midnight!

He looks back to the visits that Cooke's Circus made to Dudley between 1846 and 1849, and recalls that they opened in premises in Priory Street, later occu-

Above: The Dudley Opera House seen from the front of the Station Hotel in the 1920s. The Opera House opened on 4th. September 1899 - the brain child of John Maurice Clement (1840 -1912) who persuaded the Earl of Dudley to make the land available. Next door is a tiny cinema which began life on Christmas Eve 1910. In 1936 it was replaced with the Plaza. (Postcard in Ken Rock Colln.)

Right: The Plaza and Hippodrome stand side by side on Castle Hill in 1981. The former lasted until 1990.
The Opera house burned down in 1937 and the Hippodrome was built in its place, opening on 19th. December 1938. (NW)

Right. Not all Dudley's entertainment was centred on Castle Hill. On 3rd September 1928 the Regent opened at the top of the High Street - almost opposite Top Church. From 1950 onwards it was known as the Gaumont but closed as a cinema on 16th July 1961. It is seen here in 1981 as a Bingo & Social Club, but is now a banqueting and conference centre. (NW)

The Opera House and its successor, the Hippodrome, do not account for the entirety of Dudley's theatre history. The Colosseum in Trindle Road, and the Empire in Hall Street are also part of the story.
Left: Here we see The Empire, Hall Street as built in 1903.
The presentation of entertainment on or near this site goes back to the days of using temporary structures. Bennett & Patch had used a site in New Hall Street, various circuses had used a site a few yards away in Dudley Row. Tom Pritchard may have used a "tin circus" building before setting out to build this theatre. After all that, its theatrical life was short. It was used as a cinema from 1910 until 1940, then industrial use followed. It was demolished in 1975.
(Postcard in Ken Rock Colln.)

pied by the town gaol. He admired the equestrian skill of male and female artistes at these shows. After the circuses came the travelling shows, and once again this writer is unusual in giving them his attention and thus putting them on the record. When the Market Place was built in the centre of Dudley following the demolition of the old Town Hall which had occupied the middle of the road, he notes that shows were built up there.

Land in New Hall Street, Dudley, became available for travelling shows - including a show presented by the "celebrated tragedian": Mr. J.V. Brookes. This gentleman apparently ran a company in Dudley for a time, and shortly afterwards lost his life in a shipwreck while on his way to Australia! Wombell's Menagerie opened on the same site, when not in the Market Place.

A regular visitor to Dudley was Bennett's Show and "TB" makes the interesting claim that Mr. William Bennett was a native of Dudley. He adds the even more interesting comment that.... "Mr. William Bennett was assisted by his clever daughter, Mrs. Eliza Patch, who I now believe still conducts a theatre in Stourbridge." "TB's" comments were my introduction to the study of portable theatres in gen-

eral, and the life and times of "Bennett and Patch" in particular. As their theatre was "portable" the story is not exclusively about Dudley and will have to wait to be told elsewhere!

When we use a term like "travelling entertainment" today the example that comes most readily to mind is the "funfair". The first fair I encountered in Dudley was in Holly Hall at the Woodside Gala, but in the 1960s it was not a world that I understood. Two decades later that all began to change as I embarked on a biography of the local showman; Pat Collins. This was followed by three other books on the world of the fairground, so now feel I know it a little better. Fairs still appear in Dudley in places like Holly Hall and Buffery Park, and in recent years on the Zoo car park, and there have often been fairground amusements to be found in the Zoo itself.

There are many more fairs to account for within the present day boundaries of Dudley, but when contemplating the old pre-1966 Borough of Dudley, the principal fair - presented by Pat Collins - was on a ground just off Trindle Road, between Porter Street and Claughton Road, above the railway tunnel. It was called "The White Knobs" fairground as lime-

Many famous artistes have visited Dudley's theatres over the years, and now come to the Town Hall, re-branded as The Concert Hall.

Right: Here we see Bob Hope making his once-in-a-lifetime visit to Dudley. He presented two performances at the Hippodrome on Sunday 22nd April 1951. Bob Hope with Marilyn Maxwell at the piano pose at the theatre with Bob and Maurice Kennedy - the brothers who ran the theatre after the death of their father Ben Kennedy. Many people also recall the visits of Laurel and Hardy, but nobody is around to tell us about Dan Leno opening the Empire in 1903!

(Amy Shepherd Collection)

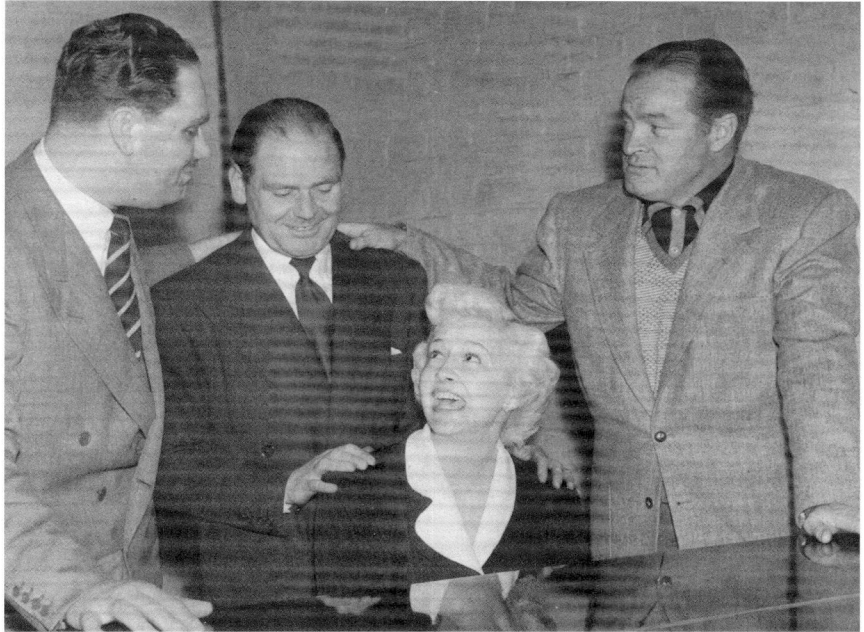

Dudley has produced its own "stars" - for example Lenny Henry in recent times. Along side the stars, the girls of Dudley's Latour Dancing School regularly appeared in pantomime at the Hippodrome. Some of the girls line up here in the 1955/56 production of "Goody Two Shoes"

(Barry Foley Collection)

Two plaques to Dudley-born stars of show business were unveiled at the Concert Hall on 21st. January 2007.

Right: Miss Mary Jane Burcher (Clarkson's PA) and Guy Higgins (of the Water Rats) unveil a plaque in memory of Clarkson Rose.

Rose (1890 - 1968) grew up in Ednam Road and became, as a child, a frequent visitor to Dudley's theatres. He became a comedian and all round entertainer - making his name as pantomime dame. He last appeared in Dudley in 1964. (NW)

As well as unveiling a plaque in memory of Clarkson Rose (see previous page), the event of 21st. January 2007 was also a tribute to Dudley's Billy Dainty. His son Larry Dainty (right) and Roy Hudd jointly unveiled this plaque. (NW)

This was followed by a tribute show in memory of Billy Dainty (1927 - 1986) starring Joan Regan and Jimmy Cricket. Above: Roy Hudd on stage before the show with Larry Dainty, Barry Balmayne and Ray Hingley. Billy grew up in Wolverhampton Street. (NW)

stone had been dumped on the surface of the ground - possibly from the days when the railway tunnel was being excavated. Such "history" might seem very esoteric but accounts of some of Pat's fairs on this ground are described in detail in the pages of World's Fair, the weekly paper of the fairground business. In the 1930s, the paper's Tipton-based reporter known as "JBT", made visits to the ground - a story I was later able to tell in "Fairs & Circuses in the Black Country".

The White Knobs Fairground played an interesting part in fairground history in 1929 while Pat was presenting a fair to accompany the newly invented Dudley Carnival. Pat was approached by a man named Jack Todd who was travelling Britain with something entirely new: The Wall of Death. Pat agreed to let Jack build up the wall on the White Knobs ground and the show took Dudley by storm. Pat was so impressed he went away and ordered Walls of Death as wedding presents for each of his four grandchildren! This moment may not compared with Roundheads laying siege to Dudley Castle during the Civil War in terms of historical importance, but I like to recall it.

The question therefore arises of whether Dudley was home to any showmen that can be identified. "JBT" provides us with an answer. In a 1936 report he pauses to reminisce about the days when Jack Hayes used to spend each winter on the White

Knobs ground. What little we know about the Hayes family tends to link them with Kates Hill in the 1890s and 1900s. They may have played a key role in organising the Kates Hill Wakes; an event very seldom reported or described - except on one occasion in 1892.

On 10th October 1892 an eleven year old boy named Henry Mountford was killed at Kates Hill Wakes when his head was struck by a swingboat. A William Taylor was apparently looking after the swingboats, and his address is given as "living in his van, based in Kates Hill." The proprietors of the swingboats are identified as Mr. & Mrs. Hayes, but they, and Mr. Taylor, were exonerated from any blame at the subsequent enquiry.

Another source of information tells us that the Hayes may have built a travelling "Ghost Show" in their Kates Hill yard, and later, in about 1901, began showing films as "The Hayes' Coronation Bioscope Show". I believe they died in the 1920s, and are buried at Ocker Hill. Maybe their story will one day be uncovered. Meanwhile I think the very mention of them illustrates how an interest in Dudley's history can change a person who once walked down Castle Hill in the early sixties, with scarcely a glance at the Hippodrome, into a present day fanatic searching for information on bygone Dudley showmen.

Right: Dudley Hippodrome was a variety theatre and as such it is true to say that a great 'variety' of shows were seen on its stage: revues, pantomime, girl-shows, local amateur operatic society shows and all kinds of concert. Here we see Captain Jerry Clarke's elephants appearing on stage as part of 'Chapman's Circus' in the 1950s
(Barry Foley)

Famous nineteenth century travelling menageries such as "Bostock & Wombells" brought their shows to Dudley Market Place, but once the tradition of presenting the circus in the "big top" was established the shows required more space. Until the Second World War, or just after, it seems that shows were presented near Birmingham Road on land that eventually became a coach park and then a car park, before disappearing under the Castle Gate Island. Since then circuses have appeared on the Zoo car park.

Mid right: Jay Millers' Circus appears on the Zoo car park in January 1989 while the trees on Castle Hill are still bare. This show is still travelling.

Lower right: Nikki Fossett presented Sir Robert Fossett's Circus on the Zoo car park in May 1992 against a greener backdrop. Nikki Fossett has gone on to present an equestrian show called "The Spirit of the Horse".

Both photographs taken from the back of the Dudley Hippodrome building. (NW)

Left: In recent years Thomas Jones' Funfair has opened on the Zoo car park early in the travelling season. (Seen here in March 2008) Although visible from the Tipton Road while the trees are bare, the site is very "tucked away". As far as it is known, no pictures of Pat Collins' fair on the White Knobs fairground near Trindle Road, have ever been found. (NW)

What do you know about skating rinks? This rink, on the corner of Trindle Road and Claughton Road, next door to the White Knobs Fairground, started life as Lloyd's Circus then became the Colosseum Theatre for John Clement, from 1889 until about 1899. Having become a skating rink in the mid 1900s, it lasted until 1921 when the old wooden building burnt down. Other Dudley rinks were to be provided next door to the Hippodrome at the foot of Castle Hill, and in the former Castle Cinema in High Street. (Ken Rock postcard colln.)

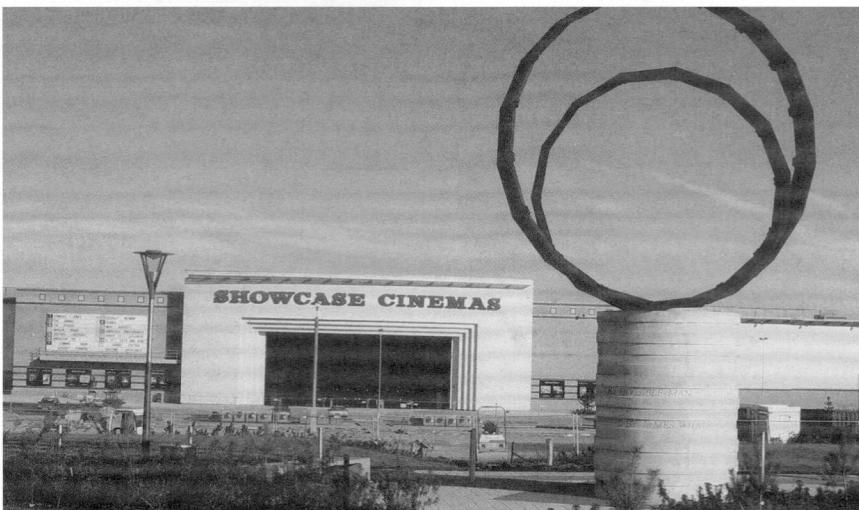

Left: The Showcase Cinema at Castle Gate - just about within the boundary of the old Borough of Dudley - on the day it opened: 12th. October 2001. The main entrance designed to reflect the style of an art-deco proscenium arch is quite grand, and in four screens Dudley citizens are offered the experience of sitting in double seats - an almost forgotten pleasure of cinema-going. (NW)

Chapter 16
Netherton

Dividing Dudley into its component parts is straightforward while dealing with the sections covered so far but when one comes to Netherton, I think it becomes more difficult, because Netherton is substantial enough to be considered on its own. It doesn't really have to be seen as part of something else. The organisation of local government in the 1890s gave places like Quarry Bank, Amblecote and Brierley Hill their own autonomy as "Urban Districts". Therefore, it seems strange at first sight that somewhere like Netherton did not receive the same recognition and status. The explanation seems to be that it was too late for such a decision to be made - Netherton had been a part of Dudley since 1865 when the borough boundary was defined. And the reason for that must go back to Netherton's association with Dudley as a detached part of Worcestershire, and all this might go back to ecclesiastical boundaries. If Netherton had been a little village in Staffordshire, like Quarry Bank, then the story might have been different.

It is difficult to recall exactly how all this looked as I made my first journey through the Black Country from Old Hill to Dudley via Netherton in the Autumn of 1962. I had no preconceived picture of Dudley let alone its surroundings - except for the reassurance of my London-based headmaster that Worcestershire was nothing but fruit orchards and rolling green hills. As I sat on the 243 bus that morning did I have a sense of where Old Hill ended and Netherton began? As I passed from Cinder Bank to Blower's Green did I have a sense of entering Dudley? Obviously not - and I was distracted by what was going on inside the bus anyway. But that does not mean that such boundaries and borders did not become clearer at a later stage.

I have already described my growing awareness of Netherton on the basis of approaching it from Holly Hall, and on the basis of discovering 101 things that are a feature of Netherton. Gradually, I also became interested in the relationship between Netherton

Below: What's a Londoner doing in Netherton? An ex London Transport "Routemaster" makes its way past the Netherton Art Centre, Northfield Road, in November 2007. (John James)

and Dudley, and have since characterised it as a "double act" called "Little and Large". At first I believed that being part of the double act was a disadvantage to Netherton, but in recent years I have come to believe that Netherton gained from being part of Dudley and that it acquired attributes that it might never have acquired had it been an isolated "urban district". On the other hand, Dudley has gained much from Netherton and many of the "Seventy Seven Wonders of Dudley" are in fact to be found in Netherton!

As soon as Dudley begins to manifest its parts: Eve Hill, Kates Hill, the Dock etc…it becomes obvious that two of the parts felt they were "more equal" than the others. These two parts are Netherton and Woodside. If central Dudley acquired something new then you can be sure that Netherton and Woodside demanded the same, whether it be a public library, a park or the arrival of electricity. Yet Netherton and Woodside did not evolve as equals. A quick look at Netherton's public hall and library compared to Woosdside's confirms that. Netherton, of all the parts of Dudley grew into the most complete township in its own right.

There are many ways of trying to understand Netherton. One way is to imagine the turnpike road of the late eighteenth century making its was from Dudley down to Halesowen and on to Bromsgrove: a highway linking centres of nail manufacture. Netherton grows up along this highway and eventually brings in other settlements on either side of it. Another way is to look at the development of the canal system. The Dudley No.1 canal and No.2 canal both exploit minor river valleys: The Black Brook and the Mousehole Sweet. These canals almost made an island of Netherton and the improvements made to the system in the 1850s really put Netherton on the map. The road and canals, the pits and the iron works create an industrial "suburb" on Dudley's doorstep. The Anglicans and the non-conformists fought for the souls of the resulting population and in no time a community grew - part of Dudley but also sufficiently self-supporting to be distinct from Dudley.

Another way of appreciating Netherton is to consider the township's own distinct and separate components: Cinder Bank, Baptist End, Windmill End, Darby End, Primrose Hill, Dudley Wood, Mushroom Green, Saltwells, The Yew Tree Hills, and Lodge Farm. However small a part of the Black Country is put under the microscope, it is soon found to divide once again into even smaller parts! Then consider the strangeness of boundaries: Cradley Heath Speedway Stadium was in Netherton, but the Netherton Canal Tunnel is actually in Rowley Regis!

In the autumn of 2004 I was launching a book about local chapels from the Sunday School building at the back of the Peoples' Mission Hall in Swan Street, Netherton, when it struck me that no one had produced a modern picture book on Netherton. This seemed an appalling 'gap' and I immediately set out to put matters right. "Netherton in Old Photographs" appeared in 2006, and "Netherton: People and Places" two years later. My work on these two books confirmed that Netherton is an interesting place and consolidated my fascination with both the township itself, and its relationship with the rest of Dudley.

My feeling is that Netherton reached its zenith in Edwardian times following the opening of the public hall and park, the arrival of Lloyds Bank and the electric trams. Some of Netherton then fell down - but that sort of thing happens in coalfields, and fine Edwardian buildings were erected in the following years. Things in Netherton just got better and better - right up until 1912 when an anchor was produced for the world's largest ship. The ship sank and Netherton eventually declined!

In 2008 Netherton has seen money spent on the park, and the "Arts Centre", there has been imaginative regeneration of living space at Canalside Walk (Bishton's Bridge) and the old Noah's Ark chapel. Plans have been drawn up for ambitious extensions to Hillcrest School & Community College, Netherton's own secondary school. The Netherton Tunnel has gloriously celebrated its 150th birthday to remind everyone of the importance of the canals and associated open spaces. If only someone had the vision to set about restoring the visual potential of the main road, we could see the regeneration of Netherton as a 'model' of the eventual regeneration of Dudley. No study of Dudley will ever be complete without paying some special attention to Netherton!

Dudley's Library and School of Art was opened in 1884. Immediately the people of Netherton and Woodside wanted their own facilities of this sort. The Countess of Dudley laid the foundation stones of both buildings on 5th July 1893 and Netherton's "Public Hall" opened a year later, containing an assembly hall with stage, a library and a reading room. A fire station and police houses completed the development.

Early in 1910 Howard Bishop began showing films in the public hall part of the building and it became known as "The Stute", or "Bungies".

On 29th August 1947 the building was relaunched as the Netherton Art Centre. (NW)

Probably the best known institution in Netherton is The Old Swan, Halesowen Road. As a home-brew pub it achieved great fame as "Ma Pardoe's" - taking its name from the landlady: Doris Pardoe. Her husband ran the pub from 1932 until 1952 when he died. Doris then kept it running until 1980. Several changes of ownership have kept the flag flying and it is now run by Tim Newey. In this 2007 picture we can see it has been extended while preserving its traditonal appearance.

The entire stretch of this road cries out for sympathetic conservation. (NW)

Recent conservation and regeneration in Netherton has included work on the fire station and police houses in Northfield Road, seen here in 2006, and the replacement of the old Savoy cinema (1936 - 1960) with a brand new community facility called The Savoy Centre which opened on 27th January 2006. Private enterprise has converted the Noahs Ark chapel which closed in 2004 into eleven new "apartments" completely preserving the exterior of the chapel and sunday school building and also using some of the interior features as well. Ayli's Cafe has now opened in the fire-station portion of this building and the success of this regeneration has to be compared with bad news from Woodside where similar buidlings seem doomed in 2008. (NW)

An important step forward in Netherton's development as an self-contained community was the arrival of Lloyd's Bank on the corner of High Street and Northfield Road in about 1902. It has now been replaced by a single storey building but is still serving Netherton.
(Roger Hodson)

Netherton's bank manager originally lived "above the bank" but did not have to look from his flat across an industrial landscape! His view looked out straight across the park - which opened about the same time as the bank - having been "reclaimed" from old wasted colliery land in an ambitious municipal scheme that carried out a similar exercise in Woodside. (Grange Park and Buffery Park were also similar schemes.)
(Roger Hodson)

Left: In the complex relationship between Netherton and the rest of Dudley, sometimes Netherton goes its own independent way, sometimes it is happy to be part Dudley. In 1929 and 1930 when Dudley organised a carnival, Netherton responded by putting on its own carnival. On the other hand, this picture, dating from 1962, illustrates the sections of the borough working together in The Festival of Queens.

Sunday Schools throughout Dudley worked on raising funds for the National Children's Homes and each elected a Queen and attendents to represent them at an event at Dudley Town Hall. Netherton Sunday Schools are being represented by Deborah Smith (later Fellows) as Queen, attended by Ann Griffin (later Smith) and Hazel Cooper (later Brown).
(Geoff and Olive Smith)

Right: Hillcrest School & Communtiy College, as Netherton's secondary school is now called, photographed in 2005.

As Dudley implemented the 1944 Education Act in the years following the war, it found itself using many old buildings, barely adequate for the job. Hillcrest School was Dudley's first purpose-built secondary school of the post-war era and opened in Simms Lane, Netherton, on 10th January 1958. It was designed by the Borough Architect, John Lewis, and was built by a local firm. Its first intake was 250 scholars from Northfield Road, later augmented by pupils from Saltwells (successor to the 'Iron Schools'.) Further such schools were built at Holly Hall and Wren's Nest. (NW)

Right: On 31st January 2008 Hillcrest celebrated its 50th Birthday with a 'party and reunion' at the school.

At this anniversary we see 'The class of 58': ex-pupils from among the first children to use the new building. Left to right: Mary Danks, Carol Chilton, Cynthia Seeley, Margaret Pritchard, Pat Beard, Janet Whitehouse and Christine Meese. (NW)

Above: Principal of Hillcrest School & Community College, Mrs. April Garratt shows the 50th Birthday cake to ex-members of staff on 31st Janaury 2008. (NW)

Left: Present scholars at Hillcrest School at the 50th Birthday Event. (NW)

Acknowledgements

A huge number of people have helped me with the production of this book, and in many cases the help goes back through the preparation of books on local chapels, on Quarry Bank, and most recently on Netherton. It would be impossible to list all those names again so I'm afraid the following list only identifies folks who have been in touch with me during the period in which this book has been prepared. Naturally I would still wish to say, "Thanks", to all the others, and anyone who gets left out.

I found particular inspiration in the work of John Stenson whose books and drawings ("Do You Remember?", "Under Boots Clock", and "Gone But Not Forgotten") pioneered a micro-history or 'step by step' approach to preserving information about Dudley. Many other books have been produced about Dudley - all of which I have probably consulted many times - ranging from Chandler & Hannah's 1949 book, "Dudley - As It Was and As It Is Today" to modern works by the folks at Dudley Archives (Hilary Atkins, Diane Mathews, Samantha Robins), plus Dr. Paul Collins and David Clare. We all owe a great debt to Edwin Blocksidge whose enthusiasm for everything to do with Dudley was poured into his annual guides.

Those who have been in contact with me while assembling this book, and who have helped me greatly include: Carolyn Arnold, Sheila Aston, Phil Barnard, Inderjit Bhogal, Deidrie Blakeway, Mabel and Jim Blewitt, Deb Brown, John Burgin and family, Eric Bytheway, Trevor and Margaret Brookes, Les & Betty Bywater, Doris Clarke, Roger Combleholme, Megan Crofts, Val Davies, Michael Dryhurst, Arthur Edwards, Kim Elwell, Mike Evans, Roy Evans, Alan George, Bernice Giles, Bill Goodman, Mavis Gorman, Michael Hale, Sue Hazelton, Frank Hensman, Dorothy Hicklin, Cynthia Ho, Sadie Hobbs, Keith Hodgkins, Roger Hodson, Professor David Hughes, Margaret Hyde, Bob Jackson, Molly James, John James, Rev. Osborn Johns, Bob Jones, Pam Ling, Bill Maiden, Eunice Maiden, Mac & Maggie McCall, Dorothy Morgan, Tony Morrall, Douglas Parker, Joan Payne, Brian Payton, Margaret Pearce, Iris Reed, Jean Richardson, Paul Roberts, Ken Rock, Joyce Round, Chris Rutter, F.B.Shaw, Lilian Sheldon, Harry Shuker, June & Vic Sidaway, Graham Sidwell, Geoff & Olive Smith, John Smith, Michael Smith, Ron Thomas, Viv and Brian Turner, Hilda Walker, Yvonne Walker, Clarice Walters, Francisca Wassell, Alan Wedge, Frank Wells, Dave Whyley, Doreen Williamson, Malcolm Woodall, Val Worwood and the Save St John's Church Group.

I am grateful for support from the Express & Star, Dudley Chronicle, Dudley News, and The Black Country Bugle plus the editor of The Blackcountryman. Information and pictures from the Dudley Archives & Local History Centre have aslo been greatly appreciated. Throughout the production of this book I have been assisted and supported by Terri Baker-Mills who co-ordinates my work-life balance.

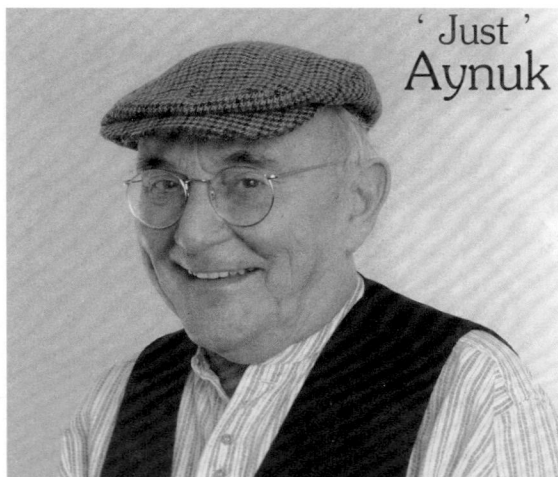

' Just '
Aynuk

And Thanks to Aynuk (Alan Smith), seen on the left, for launching this book on 15th November 2008 at Central Methodist Church, Dudley.
(Trevor Owen Photography)